Closing the Loop

Assessing and Teaching Striving Readers

SUZANNE M. ROSE, PH. D.

SLIPPERY ROCK UNIVERSITY OF PENNSYLVANIA

Kendall Hunt
publishing company

Cover images © Shutterstock, Inc.

Kendall Hunt
publishing company

www.kendallhunt.com
Send all inquiries to:
4050 Westmark Drive
Dubuque, IA 52004-1840

Copyright © 2019 by Kendall Hunt Publishing Company

ISBN: 978-1-5249-8484-7

Published in the United States of America

Contents

PART I

The Basics

Identifying Students with Reading Difficulties

Screening Assessments to Identify At-Risk Students

Screening tools are assessments that provide a means for identifying children who may be at risk for failure in learning to read and write. Teachers typically administer the screening tool to all students in a class, so these assessments tend to be quick to administer and easy to score.

Typically, screening assessments are used in conjunction with *benchmarks* and a *progress monitoring system* in order to determine and track student growth over time.

One example of widely used screening instruments are the DIBELS group of assessments. DIBELS, the Dynamic Indicators of Basic Early Literacy Skills assessments, originated in 1999 at the University of Oregon. DIBELS is a set of assessments for students in grades K-6. As with all screening tools, the purpose of DIBELS is to identify students who are at risk for problems with literacy development (DIBELS, 2013).

The DIBELS assessments can be used to gather data about students' development in the areas of phonemic awareness, phonics, fluency, vocabulary, and comprehension. DIBELS assessments are administered three times each year. Following each assessment, the teacher compares student scores with benchmark scores to determine whether or not each student is making adequate progress in the target skills. Students who do not meet the benchmark scores for the assessments are targeted for additional support and instruction; these students are also monitored closely (progress monitoring) and are assessed repeatedly on the target skills— sometimes once each week.

Although DIBELS is widely used in thousands of schools, mostly due to the fact that it is inexpensive and quick, it is also very controversial. Much of the controversy about the use of DIBELS stems from criticisms about whether the content of the assessments actually reflects authentic reading skills. In addition, most of the DIBELS assessments take only one minute to administer, leaving many literacy professionals doubting their ability to accurately assess students' actual levels of development. Finally, there is much criticism that the additional instruction received by the at-risk students who are identified by the DIBELS assessments is targeted at passing the next assessment rather than building students' actual literacy development.

There are many other literacy screening tools available; some are informal tools and others are commercially available. One other common literacy screening tool is the PALS series of assessments. PALS stands for Phonological Awareness Literacy Screening. According to the publisher, PALS assessments are used in all 50 states and in several foreign countries (PALS, 2013). There are three different PALS series—PALS-PreK, PALS-K, and PALS 1-3. The PALS assessments are similar to DIBELS; the assessments provide data, which are then compared to the provided benchmarks so that students who are at risk for literacy difficulties can be identified and provided with additional instructional opportunities.

Discrepancy Model

The *discrepancy model* is an approach for identifying students who are not performing at an expected level on literacy tasks. Unlike screening instruments, which rely on benchmark data to identify at-risk students, the discrepancy model allows teachers to calculate specific expectations for individual students, based on each student's chronological age and IQ. This approach, recommended by Harris and Sipay, is based on the comparison of the student's potential reading performance with his actual performance.

Through the use of the discrepancy model, one can determine whether or not a student has a reading problem by following this process:

1. Compute the student's *reading age (RA)*. To do this, add 5.2 to the student's reading grade-equivalent score that was obtained from her most recent standardized reading assessment.

$$\text{Reading age (RA)} = \text{Reading grade equivalent} + 5.2$$

2. Since this process involves mathematical manipulation of the data, it is necessary to have all the data in the same format. A student's *chronological age (CA)* is reported in years and months, and there are 12 months in a year; to utilize this information in calculations, it must be converted from years and months to decimal format (years and tenths).

   Use the chart below to convert the CA from years and months to a decimal format.

1 month = .1	5 months = .4	9 months = .75
2 months = .2	6 months = .5	10 months = .8
3 months = .25	7 months = .6	11 months = .9
4 months = .3	8 months = .7	

   For example, if Alejandro is 7 years and 7 months old, for subsequent calculations, you would use the decimal 7.6. If he was 9 years and 10 months old, you would use 9.8.

3. Compute the *mental age (MA)* using the chronological age (in decimal format, *not* in years and months) and the student's reported IQ score.

$$\text{Mental age (MA)} = \frac{\text{CA} \times \text{IQ}}{100}$$

4. Determine the student's *reading expectancy age (RExpA)* using this equation:

$$\text{Reading expectancy age (RExpA)} = \frac{2\,\text{MA} + \text{CA}}{3}$$

5. Compare the student's reading age (RA) and reading expectancy age (RExpA) to determine the difference between the student's actual achievement and his expected achievement. Use this formula to make the comparison:

   reading expectancy age (RExpA) – reading age (RA) = Difference
   (difference between expected achievement and actual achievement)

6. To determine whether the student has a reading problem or whether the difference is a "tolerable difference," compare the calculated difference with the following chart, first developed by Wilson and Cleland in 1985:

If the child is at the end of this grade level:	The "tolerable difference" is:
Grade 1	0.5 year
Grade 2	0.5 year
Grade 3	0.5 year
Grade 4	1 year
Grade 5	1 year
Grade 6	1 year
Grade 7	1.5 years
Grade 8	1.5 years
Grade 9	1.5 years
Grade 10	2 years
Grade 11	2 years
Grade 12	2 years

Because calculating the reading expectancy age and reading age can be cumbersome and time-consuming, Mariotti and Homan (2005) developed a table to assist teachers in quickly determining a student's reading expectancy grade level. To determine whether or not a student has a reading problem using the table, simply locate the closest chronological age (CA) in years and months (no conversion required!) and then move across the line to the student's IQ score. The reading expectancy grade level is the spot where the two lines intersect. See Figure 1 to use the chart.

Critics of the discrepancy model argue that using students' IQs results in lower expectations for some students. For example, two students who are both 8 years 4 months of age will not be expected to achieve at the same level—if one has an IQ of 100 and the other has an IQ of 135, the student with the higher IQ will be expected to be more advanced. Similarly, a student with a below-average IQ would not be expected to be achieving as much as other students of the same age or grade level. Proponents of the discrepancy approach believe this is realistic; students have differing abilities and should be expected to perform differently at the same age. Opponents disagree, arguing that all children should be performing "on grade level," regardless of their IQ.

RTI Model

Response to Intervention (RtI) is a model for instruction that is based on the use of universal screening, progress monitoring, and the use of tiered instruction.

Tier 1: General Education Program

Instruction provided at Tier 1 involves the use of an evidence-based, scientifically researched core instructional program (Shapiro, 2013). This is the main curriculum adopted by the school;

for example, in literacy instruction, this would include the adopted reading series, spelling program, and writing curriculum. The belief is that if the core program is implemented effectively, at least 75 to 80 percent of students will be performing at the expected level. All children in a classroom receive Tier 1 instruction; those who do not perform as expected are identified as "at risk" or "at high risk" and receive supplemental instruction in Tier 2 or Tier 3 activities. The instruction received in Tiers 2 and 3 is differentiated to better meet students' needs.

Tier 2: Small-Group Intervention

Tier 2 interventions are usually conducted in groups of five to eight students who have not made adequate achievement as a result of Tier 1 instruction. Instruction provided may be differentiated in terms of intensity, length, materials, and provided support.

Tier 3: Intensive Intervention

Tier 3 interventions are usually conducted in smaller groups three to five students, or, in some cases, Tier 3 may involve 1:1 instruction. Students who do not respond adequately to Tier 3 activities will be considered potential candidates for identification as having special education needs.

Chronological Age (years.months)	IQ Score														
	70	75	80	85	90	95	100	105	110	115	120	125	130	135	140	145
6.0	---	---	---	---	---	---	---	1.0	1.2	1.4	1.6	1.8	2.0	2.2	2.4	2.6
6.3	---	---	---	---	---	---	1.0	1.2	1.5	1.7	1.9	2.1	2.3	2.5	2.7	2.9
6.6	---	---	---	---	---	1.1	1.3	1.5	1.7	2.0	2.2	2.4	2.6	2.8	3.0	3.2
6.9	---	---	---	---	1.1	1.3	1.6	1.8	2.0	2.2	2.4	2.7	2.9	3.1	3.4	3.6
7.0	---	---	---	1.1	1.3	1.6	1.8	2.0	2.3	2.5	2.7	3.0	3.2	3.4	3.7	3.9
7.3	---	---	1.1	1.3	1.6	1.8	2.0	2.3	2.5	2.8	3.0	3.2	3.5	3.7	4.0	4.2
7.6	---	1.0	1.3	1.6	1.8	2.0	2.3	2.6	2.8	3.0	3.3	3.6	3.8	4.0	4.3	4.6
7.9	1.0	1.3	1.5	1.8	2.0	2.3	2.6	2.8	3.1	3.3	3.6	3.8	4.1	4.4	4.6	4.9
8.0	1.2	1.5	1.7	2.0	2.3	2.5	2.8	3.1	3.3	3.6	3.9	4.1	4.4	4.7	4.9	5.2
8.3	1.4	1.7	2.0	2.2	2.5	2.8	3.0	3.3	3.6	3.9	4.2	4.4	4.7	5.1	5.3	5.5
8.6	1.6	1.9	2.2	2.4	2.7	3.0	3.3	3.6	3.9	4.2	4.4	4.7	5.0	5.3	5.6	5.8
8.9	1.8	2.1	2.4	2.7	3.0	3.3	3.6	3.8	4.1	4.4	4.7	5.0	5.3	5.6	5.9	6.2
9.0	2.0	2.3	2.6	2.9	3.2	3.5	3.8	4.1	4.4	4.7	5.0	5.3	5.6	5.9	6.2	6.5
9.3	2.2	2.5	2.8	3.1	3.4	3.7	4.0	4.4	4.7	5.0	5.3	5.6	5.9	6.2	6.5	6.8
9.6	2.4	2.7	3.0	3.4	3.7	4.0	4.3	4.6	4.9	5.2	5.6	5.9	6.2	6.5	6.8	7.2
9.9	2.6	2.9	3.2	3.6	3.9	4.2	4.6	4.9	5.2	5.5	5.8	6.2	6.5	6.8	7.2	7.5
10.0	2.8	3.1	3.5	3.8	4.1	4.5	4.8	5.1	5.5	5.8	6.1	6.5	6.8	7.1	7.5	7.8
10.3	3.0	3.3	3.7	4.0	4.4	4.7	5.0	5.4	5.7	6.1	6.4	6.8	7.1	7.4	7.8	8.1
10.6	3.2	3.6	3.9	4.2	4.6	5.0	5.3	5.6	6.0	6.4	6.7	7.0	7.4	7.8	8.1	8.4
10.9	3.4	3.8	4.1	4.5	4.8	5.2	5.6	5.9	6.3	6.6	7.0	7.3	7.7	8.1	8.4	8.8
11.0	3.6	4.0	4.3	4.7	5.1	5.4	5.8	6.2	6.5	6.9	7.3	7.6	8.0	8.4	8.7	9.1
11.3	3.8	4.2	4.6	4.9	5.3	5.7	6.0	6.4	6.8	7.2	7.6	7.9	8.3	8.7	9.0	9.4
11.6	4.0	4.4	4.8	5.2	5.5	5.9	6.3	6.7	7.1	7.4	7.8	8.2	8.6	9.0	9.4	9.8
11.9	4.2	4.6	5.0	5.4	5.8	6.2	6.6	7.0	7.3	7.7	8.1	8.5	8.9	9.3	9.7	10.1
12.0	4.4	4.8	5.2	5.6	6.0	6.4	6.8	7.2	7.6	8.0	8.4	8.8	9.2	9.6	10.0	10.4
12.3	4.6	5.0	5.4	5.8	6.2	6.6	7.0	7.4	7.9	8.3	8.7	9.1	9.5	9.9	10.3	10.7
12.6	4.8	5.2	5.6	6.0	6.5	6.9	7.3	7.7	8.1	8.6	9.0	9.4	9.8	10.2	10.6	11.0
12.9	5.0	5.4	5.8	6.3	6.7	7.1	7.6	8.0	8.4	8.8	9.2	9.7	10.1	10.5	11.0	11.4
13.0	5.2	5.6	6.1	6.5	6.9	7.4	7.8	8.2	8.7	9.1	9.5	10.0	10.4	10.8	11.3	11.7
13.3	5.4	5.8	6.3	6.7	7.2	7.6	8.0	8.5	8.9	9.4	9.8	10.2	10.7	11.1	11.5	12.0
13.6	5.6	6.0	6.5	7.0	7.4	7.8	8.3	8.8	9.2	9.6	10.1	10.5	11.0	11.4	11.9	12.4
13.9	5.8	6.3	6.7	7.2	7.6	8.1	8.6	9.0	9.5	9.9	10.4	10.8	11.3	11.8	12.2	12.7
14.0	6.0	6.5	6.9	7.4	7.9	8.3	8.8	9.3	9.7	10.2	10.7	11.1	11.6	12.1	12.5	13.0
14.3	6.2	6.7	7.2	7.6	8.1	8.6	9.0	9.5	10.0	10.5	11.0	11.4	11.9	12.4	12.8	13.3
14.6	6.4	6.9	7.4	7.8	8.3	8.8	9.3	9.8	10.3	10.8	11.2	11.7	12.2	12.7	13.2	13.6
14.9	6.6	7.1	7.6	8.1	8.6	9.1	9.6	10.0	10.5	11.0	11.5	12.0	12.5	13.0	13.5	14.0
15.0	6.8	7.3	7.8	8.3	8.8	9.3	9.8	10.3	10.8	11.3	11.8	12.3	12.8	13.3	13.8	14.3

Figure 1.1   Reading Expectancy Grade Table

(adapted from Mariotti and Homan, 2005)

Chapter Activities

1. Use the discrepancy model and the degree of tolerable difference to determine whether each of these students may have a reading problem.
   Show your calculations.
   a. Mary has a chronological age of 7 years 3 months. Her score on the California Achievement Test indicated a reading achievement level of first grade, third month. She obtained an IQ score of 120 on the WISC-III. Mary is in second grade. Does Mary have a reading discrepancy? If yes, is it a significant difference?
   b. Juan has a chronological age of 10 years 2 months. His score on the Metropolitan Achievement Test indicated a reading achievement level of fourth grade, seventh month. He obtained a score of 85 on the WISC-III. Juan is in fourth grade. Does he have a reading discrepancy? If yes, is it a significant one?
   c. Bob has a chronological age of 12 years 5 months. His score on the Metropolitan Achievement test, taken in April of sixth grade, indicated a reading achievement level of sixth grade, seventh month. Bob's IQ, according to the Stanford-Binet IV Intelligence Test, is 132. Does Bob have a reading discrepancy? If yes, is it a significant one?
2. Use the reading expectancy grade table in Figure 3.1 to complete these activities.
   a. Li has a CA of 10 years 2 months. His IQ score is 100. His independent reading level on the Stieglitz IRI was fourth grade and instructional level was fifth grade. Does Li have a reading discrepancy? If yes, is it a significant one?
   b. Allison has a chronological age of six years, two months. Her score on the California Achievement Test indicated a reading achievement level of first grade, seventh month. She is in first grade. Her score on the WISC-III indicated an IQ of 120. Does Allison have a reading discrepancy? If yes, is it a significant one?

References

DIBELS Data System. (2013). Retrieved from: https://dibels.uoregon.edu/

Harris, A.J. & Sipay, E.R. (1985). *How to Increase Reading Ability: A Guide to Developmental and Remedial Methods*. NY: Longman.

Jennings, J.H., et al. (2010). *Reading Problems: Assessment & Teaching Strategies*. Boston: Allyn & Bacon.

Mariotti, A.S. & Homan, S.P. (2005). *Linking Reading Assessment to Instruction*. Mahwah, NJ: Lawrence Erlbaum.

PALS (2013). Retrieved from: https://www.palsmarketplace.com/assessments

Shapiro, E.S. (2013). Tiered Instruction and Intervention in a Response-to-Intervention Model. RTI Action Network. Retrieved from: http://www.rtinetwork.org/essential/tieredinstruction/tiered-instruction-and-intervention-rti-model

Wilson, R.M. & Cleland, C.J. (1990*). Diagnostic and Remedial Reading for Classroom and Clinic*. Prentice-Hall.

Differentiating Literacy Instruction

Differentiating Instruction

Differentiating instruction to meet the varying strengths and needs of all students is a vital aspect to effective instruction and is also an underlying premise of the tiered instructional approach that is part of the Response-to-Intervention model. This chapter will explore a variety of ways that teachers can modify content, process, and products in the classroom to differentiate instruction to meet the needs of all students.

Differentiating Content

One method of differentiating literacy instruction for students is to vary the content with which the students are working. This can be accomplished through the use of the following:

- Texts on different reading levels (text sets)
- Texts in different formats (graphic novels, magazines, books)
- Texts with differing levels of conceptual density
- Content "packaged" in different formats, such as the use of learning contracts or mini-lessons
- A variety of supported instruction approaches, including books on tape, partner reading, or 1:1 tutoring
- Modifications of the amount of material or content with which students are working (e.g., number of spelling words or chapters to read)
- Student choice (topic, content, format)

When working with textbooks in the classroom, teachers can differentiate content by:

- Supplementing texts with newspapers, trade books, poems, and other texts
- Developing a "reading road map" guide to support students' reading of the textbook
- Creating mini-textbooks by cutting apart old textbooks and creating one-chapter mini-books that will not overwhelm striving readers. Laminating these books can enable the use of highlighting instructional strategies without permanently ruining the text.

Differentiating Process

In addition to differentiating content, teachers can also vary the instructional processes or activities students complete when interacting with the content. Some suggestions for differentiating process include the following:

- Games
- Manipulatives
- Computers and other technology
- Working with partners or small groups
- Literacy centers with varied tasks
- Activities modified to support learning styles preferences
- Using flexible grouping or varied degrees of scaffolding
- Allowing for student activity choices
- Provide guide sheets, visual aids, flow charts, or models

- "Frontload" the activity by preteaching certain information
- Use cooperative learning approaches (e.g., jigsaw, literature circles)
- Vary the length and frequency of direct instruction

Differentiating Products

A third way to differentiate literacy instruction is to differentiate the products that students produce as a result of the learning activities in which they are engaged. Some alternatives for differentiating products are as follows:

- Giving verbal responses instead of written ones
- Making a drawing instead of writing an essay
- Allowing students to choose their preferred product to demonstrate learning (e.g., poem, play, poster, dance, diorama, and song)
- Varying the requirements of the completed project (e.g., essay with fewer pages)

Addressing Learning Styles

Students have a variety of learning styles and strengths. Trying to address the needs of each student in the classroom can be a challenge. This chapter will present some ideas for accommodating and addressing a variety of learning styles in the classroom, through classroom organization, differentiated instructional strategies, and differentiated materials.

Tomlinson identified some basic tenets of a differentiated classroom. These include the following (1999, p. 48):

- The teacher is clear about what matters in subject matter.
- The teacher understands, appreciates, and builds upon student differences.
- Assessment and instruction are inseparable.
- The teacher adjusts content, process, and product in response to student readiness, interests, and learning profile.
- All students participate in respectful work.
- Students and teachers are collaborators in learning.
- Goals of a differentiated classroom are maximum growth and individual success.
- Flexibility is the hallmark of a differentiated classroom.

Classroom Organization

One basic step in addressing the wide variety of students' learning styles is to consider the organization of the classroom. The classroom environment should be designed so that, as much as possible, it provides alternatives that will address students' needs.

According to Dunn and Dunn, teachers should consider including these areas in their classrooms so that the greatest number of student learning styles are addressed (1999, p. 78–79):

- Areas in the classroom that can be used by several students at the same time for the purpose of discussing what is being learned

- Reading areas that are well-lit, such as comfy reading chairs or a reading corner near the windows or with additional lighting that students may choose to use if they prefer a brighter environment
- Warmer areas that can be chosen as work spaces, such as areas near the windows or classroom heat source
- Cooler areas that can be chosen as work spaces, such as areas away from the classroom heat source
- Work areas featuring desks as well as those with tables and chairs so that students can select to work alone or in a small group
- Classroom areas where responsible students can opt to work without direct supervision
- Classroom areas that provide flexible space that would allow for students to work comfortably alone, in pairs, in small groups, with an adult, or in any combination thereof, such as modular tables that can be formed into a variety of shapes and sizes
- Screened or otherwise private and relatively quiet study areas for individual students or pairs of students, such as study carrels or large appliance boxes with one side removed
- Classroom areas that are darker or which can be darkened for media viewing, photography, or dramatizations
- Carpeted, informal areas with comfy furniture, such as bean bags, a couch, or upholstered chairs
- Classroom work areas that permit close supervision of less responsible students, such as areas near the teacher's desk
- A classroom work area where snacking is permitted

Teachers can utilize a variety of materials and furniture to create these sections of the classroom. Bookcases, pianos, carts, and easels are often useful for dividing spaces while still providing clear sight lines for the teacher to supervise activities in all areas of the classroom.

Differentiated Instructional Strategies and Materials

In addition to classroom organization, teachers can address students' learning modalities by differentiating the instructional strategies and materials they use with their students. While not an exhaustive list, the following suggestions are options for meeting students' learning needs:

Visual Learners
Movies
Computer-based games
Word hunts (not word finds!) with clipboards
Red/Green signals for reinforcing left to right
Word configuration activities
Word Wall activities
Highlighting tape or highlighting markers
Eyelighters
Flashlights for word walls
Color-coded cards to support learning material that can be grouped
Environmental print, posters
Individual white boards/chalkboards

Photographs and visual art (paintings, sculpture, mobiles, murals)
Charts and graphs (such as bar graphs, pie graphs, line graphs, etc.)
Graphic organizers (such as word maps, semantic maps, plot maps, etc.)
Anchor charts, bookmarks, posters
Books, magazines, graphic novels
Flashcards

Auditory Learners

Scaffolded spelling ("stretching words," etc.)
Object sorts (sort objects according to beginning/ending sounds)
Elkonin boxes
Think alouds
Verbalized routines, such as for writing letters or numbers
Echo reading
Jigsaw cooperative learning activities
Book discussion groups, literature circles
Books on tape/CD
Raps, chants, poems, songs, fingerplays
Earphone for reading to oneself (PVC pipe)

Kinesthetic/Tactile Learners

Shower curtain games
Board games
Relay games
Card games
Simulations
Pantomimes
3-D displays and dioramas
Jigsaw puzzles
Learning centers with manipulatives
Becoming the information to be learned (e.g., acting out the water cycle)
Being the word/Being the letter
Word sorting, picture sorting
VIP/INSERT
Sticky notes
Magnetic letters, letter tiles, word tiles, onset/rime tiles, letter dice
Wands, pointers, etc. for word walls
Sandpaper letters, salt boxes for tracing, shaving cream, fingerpaints
Puppets

Varying Entry Points

The idea of addressing students' varied learning styles and multiple intelligences through providing varying entry points (also called "windows") to the content was developed by Howard Gardner; it was first outlined in his book, *The Unschooled Mind* (1991). Gardner outlined five potential entry points that teachers could use to initiate lessons; each entry point appeals to a different learning style. According to Strickland (2013), the entry points described by Gardner are as follows:

- **Narrational Window**
  Introducing the lesson/content by reading a story or other narrative
- **Logical-Quantitative Window**
  Introducing the lesson/content through the use of data, deductive reasoning, statistics, musical rhythm, logic, narrative plot structure, cause-and-effect relationships
- **Foundational Window**
  Using basic vocabulary terms and underlying philosophy of the content or topic; in other words, focus on the "big picture"
- **Aesthetic Window**
  Focusing on the sensory or tactile features
- **Experiential Window**
  Using a hands-on activity, dealing directly with materials (physically or virtually), simulations, personal explanations

Possible ideas for using varied entry points/windows include the following:

Narrational Window Activities

Read stories about the topic.
Write about students' personal experiences related to the topic.
Write or discuss students' connections to the topic.
Tell stories related to students' experiences with the topic.
Read biographies of famous individuals connected to the content.
Read other texts by the same author, and discuss style/use of traits,
Use invented dialogues/interviews with individuals connected to content.
Case studies.

Logical-Quantitative Window Activities

Examine statistics related to the topic.
Look at patterns related to the content.
Do an experiment related to the topic.
Examine cause-and-effect relationships within the content.
Create timelines of significant events related to the topic.
Create graphic organizers to show interrelationships among topics.

Foundational Window Activities

Use a predictogram to work with content-related vocabulary before the lesson.
Examine content-related vocabulary for similar origins/roots (etymology).
Complete word sorts using content-related vocabulary.
Select important quotes from a text and explain their importance.
Explain why the topic under study is personally important.

Aesthetic Window Activities

Create drawings or paintings illustrating the topic.
Read or write poetry related to the content.

Listen to music that portrays some aspect of the content.

View dance, drama, or visual art related to the topic.

Watch videos or movies that are content related.

Listen to interviews with individuals associated with the content.

Experiential Window Activities

Take field trips to sites related to the topic.

Build models or dioramas.

Participate in simulations of content-related activities.

Complete a story tableau.

Become the content (i.e., students become the parts of solar system).

For instruction to be effective, it is critical that teachers recognize that the goals of the instruction can be realized through a large number of activities or experiences. Varying the instructional experiences in the classroom, according to students' learning preferences, provides more support for student learning and ensures that each student can access the information.

Chapter Activities

1. Identify a content area topic (mathematics, social studies, science, health) that would be taught in third grade. Locate reading materials that you could use to provide differentiation in content for students in a typical third grade, with a reading level range of preprimer to sixth grade. Find at least five different texts you could use for this class.
   a. List at least one content standard that relates to the topic you have selected.
   b. List each of the texts you have selected. Provide a complete bibliographic citation and the reading level for each text.

2. Select a literacy-related instructional activity appropriate for fourth-grade students. Explain how you could modify the content, process, and products used in activity to meet students' needs for more support or less support. Fill in the chart to indicate the variations you would use in the classroom.

	Most Support (striving students)	Middle (average students)	Least Support (advanced students)
Content			
Process			
Products			

3. Select a literacy-related activity that you have used in the past. Use the information in this chapter, as well as any additional resources related to learning styles that you have available, to modify the activity so that it specifically addresses each of the learning modalities (visual, auditory, kinesthetic/tactile).
   a. Specifically, what revisions would you make in the activity to address each learning style?
   b. Explain how each of your revisions addresses a particular learning style.

4. Do some research using online and printed resources to identify two additional literacy-related instructional strategies for each of the learning modalities. List the strategies you find in the chart below.

	Instructional Strategy #1	Instructional Strategy #2
Visual		
Auditory		
Kinesthetic/Tactile		

5. Assume the role of a third-grade teacher who is planning to teach the class about the ocean. Brainstorm at least one entry point/window activity that could be used for each of the five types of entry points. Be specific with your activity ideas—for example, don't write that you will "read a book about the ocean" but indicate specifically what book you will read.

6. Read both tasks below. Brainstorm ideas for ways to revise each activity so that it meets the same goal(s) but provides additional support for the students at each tier in RTI. Rewrite each task for each tier so that it provides the appropriate level of support. Explain your choices for each tier.

   a. **Slice and Spice Task**
      Students "slice" out an interesting part of a familiar story. Using that slice as the middle of a new story, they write a new beginning and a new ending, adding additional details and at least two new events. Text: *Tonight on the Titanic* by M.P. Osborne Lexile: 340

   b. **Predictogram Task**
      Students sort 18 words into given story element categories (characters, setting, etc.). They then use the words to write a prediction about what the story will be about. Text: *Tonight on the Titanic* by M.P. Osborne Lexile: 340

References

Forsten, C.; Grant, J.; & Hollas, B. (2003). *Differentiating Textbooks: Strategies to Improve Student Comprehension & Motivation.* Peterborough, NH: Crystal Spring Books.

Gardner, H. (1991). *The Unschooled Mind.* NY: Basic Books.

Opitz, M.F. & Ford, M. P. (2008). *Do-Able Differentiation: Varying Groups, Texts, and Supports to Reach Readers.* Portsmouth, NH: Heinemann.

Strickland, C. (2013). *The Five Entry Points of Howard Gardner.* Retrieved from: http://dilangley .wikispaces.com/file/view/bENTRY+POINTS+2009+sec.pdf

Tomlinson, C.A. (1999). *The Differentiated Classroom: Responding to the Needs of All Learners.* Alexandria, VA: ASCD.

Informal Formative Assessment

Informal Formative Assessment: Checking for Understanding

A critical aspect of teaching is to determine whether or not the students understand what has been taught and have learned from the lesson or activity. How do teachers know whether students have met the lesson objectives? Asking students, "Are there any questions?" does not work; they will rarely ask, even if they have many questions. Assessments that occur at the end of a lesson are often used for this purpose; however, they are not enough. Effective teachers also utilize assessment throughout a lesson to continuously monitor students' learning at each stage of the lesson. This allows teachers to *check for understanding* so that they can modify their teaching, if needed, to support students' success. For example, if a teacher knows that the students are not understanding what has been taught, he or she may give additional examples, provide additional guided practice, incorporate modeling or a hands-on activity, and so on. This process is also called *monitoring and adjusting* teaching to meet students' needs.

Formative assessments are administered *during* instruction to:

- Help teachers identify *which students* have learned the content/skill being taught and *how well* the students have learned so that the teacher may plan the next step in the instructional process
- Assist students in self-assessing their understanding of the new content/skill

Formative assessments should be planned in advance and included in the lesson plan. Some teachers include a formative assessment column along the right margin of each lesson plan. In this column, they indicate the specific questions or activities students will complete at each part of the lesson to demonstrate their understanding. In addition, teachers may note additional examples or questions that they plan to use if the students are still struggling with the content.

Gathering Data through Active Student Engagement

Research has repeatedly documented that students who are actively engaged in a lesson or instructional activity learn more than those students who are not. This seems like common sense; however, many teachers do not consider this when engaged in lesson planning. Read through the two activities described below. In which activity are all of the students actively engaged in the learning?

Lesson objective: After reading a story, TLW correctly identify the characters and setting (time and place).

Activity 1: After reading a story in the reading anthology, Mrs. Smith calls on individual students in her first-grade class to identify the main characters and setting of the story.

Activity 2: After reading a story in the reading anthology, Mrs. Smith gives each first-grade student three cards that read: *who, when, where*. She then puts a word card into the pocket chart, has the students choral read the card with her, and then asks the students to hold up the correct card to identify whether the word on her card indicates *who, when,* or *where* in the story.

Notice that in the second activity, all the students are actively engaged in all aspects of the lesson. Mrs. Smith can glance around the room at the cards selected by the students and can tell immediately whether the majority of the class has understood the lesson. In addition, she can pinpoint specific students who may be in need of individual or small group practice. Activities like this also provide the teacher with the data needed to adjust instruction in the next stage of the lesson. If Mrs. Smith sees that the majority of the students are incorrectly identifying the characters or setting, she knows that she will need to reteach that part of the lesson before allowing the students to practice independently. In this situation, she might utilize the additional examples or activities she has included in her lesson plan for this purpose. She also might decide that she will reteach the lesson the following day. Without information gathered from formative assessment, Mrs. Smith would not be aware that this reteaching or review was needed.

Ideas for Integrating Informal Formative Assessment into Lessons

There are myriad ways to actively involve students in lessons while gathering formative assessment data to check for understanding and to monitor and adjust teaching. Specific approaches vary from grade to grade and subject to subject, but what they all have in common is that they require the active involvement of each student. Some of the most popular approaches for checking for understanding include the following:

Individual White Boards

Students each use individual white boards and erasable markers (or chalkboards and chalk) to respond to the teacher's questions, to demonstrate that they can solve posed problems, or to provide other requested information.

Index Cards

Students make or are given several cards, which they can use to respond to the teacher's questions. This approach works well for activities in which there are a finite number of responses from which the students can choose. For example, a teacher may give students three or four cards from which to choose. If there are more than four possible responses, it is best to use a white board. One benefit of using index cards is that it takes less time for the students to choose and hold up a card than it takes for them to write out a response on a white board.

Hand Signals

Hand signals work well when there are only one or two possible responses. For example, a teacher may ask students to give a thumbs up or thumbs down to indicate whether two given words are homophones. Other creative hand signals may be used for lessons, such as having the students form a letter V with their fingers when the teacher displays a letter that is a vowel and a letter C when a consonant is displayed. Students may also be asked to use thumbs up or thumbs down to indicate whether or not they agree with a fellow classmate's response.

Fist-to-Five

Students may be asked to demonstrate their level of understanding of a topic by doing a fist-to-five response. Students who do not understand the topic at all hold up a fist, students who barely understand hold up one finger, and so on. A student who is confident that he or she completely understands would hold up all five fingers.

Thumb-o-Meter

Similar to *fist-to-five*, students are taught to use their thumbs to display their level of agreement or confidence. If a student completely agrees with a response, he or she gives a thumbs up. If the student is unsure or only partially agrees, he or she holds the thumb sideways (like a hitchhiker). Students who completely disagree give a thumbs down.

Glass, Bugs, Mud

Students are taught to think about seeing through a car's windshield. When the windshield is completely clear, they can easily see through the glass. If the car has been driven for a while and there are many bugs stuck on the windshield, it is more difficult to see and is not as clear. If the car has been driven through the mud and the windshield is covered, the windshield is not at all clear. After learning the analogy, students can be asked to raise their hands to indicate whether their understanding of a point or idea is glass (clear), bugs (a little fuzzy), or mud (not clear at all).

Red Light, Green Light

Similar to *clear, bugs, mud*, students use red, yellow, or green to indicate their level of readiness to move on to the next stage of the lesson or their level of understanding. The teacher can give them squares of colored paper, popsicle sticks, or other manipulatives to hold up or place on their desks to show whether they are ready (green), need a little help (yellow), or are not at all ready (red.) These types of markers can also be used when teachers are working with small groups and students are working independently. The students can display the correct colored card on their desks as they work. When the teacher has time in-between groups or while the small group is working on a task, he or she can glance quickly around the room to see which students are in need of his or her assistance.

Four Corners

The teacher poses a question for the students, and the students must select one of four possible answers that are displayed in the corners of the room. Students go to stand near the answer of their choice and then discuss the response with the others in their group to clarify their understanding regarding why they selected that response.

Accountable Talk

Accountable talk, developed by Lauren Resnick, is a framework that should be taught to students so that they know how to engage in partner conversations during a lesson. These partner conversations may include *turn-and-talk* or *think-pair-share* activities that will actively engage students in the lesson and provide teachers with formative feedback about student understanding. According to Fisher and Frey (2007), students using accountable talk are taught that, when engaged in partner conversations, they should:

- Stay on topic.
- Use information that is accurate and appropriate for the topic.
- Think deeply about what the partner has to say.

Whip Around

Whip around is a formative assessment activity that can be effectively used as closure for a lesson. The teacher asks the students a question that encompasses the gist of the lesson, typically one that has multiple responses, such as "What are the characteristics of mammals?" Students then jot down three responses to the question. When they have finished writing, they stand up. The teacher then randomly calls on individual students to share one of the responses on their list. As that student shares, the other students check off that response if it appears on their lists. Students sit down when all of their responses have been said, whether or not they were the ones to state them to the class. The activity ends when all the students are sitting down. This process allows the teacher to quickly determine whether the students learned the main points of the lesson.

Retelling or Summarizing

Having students retell or summarize what they have read, heard, or viewed is an effective way to check for understanding.

References

Fisher, D. & Frey, N. (2007). Checking for Understanding: Formative Assessment Techniques for Your Classroom. Alexandria, VA: ASCD.

Newman, L. & Flaherty, S. (2012). Checking for Understanding: Key Assessment for Learning Techniques. *Expeditionary Learning*, 1–3.

CHAPTER 4

Standardized Assessments

Characteristics of Standardized Literacy Assessments

A *standardized assessment* is one that is administered under the same conditions for every test-taker—in other words, the standards for administering the assessment are consistent from administration to administration of the assessment. Standardized assessments provide specific instructions for the administrators to follow; varying from these instructions invalidates the scores that are obtained. For example, a standardized assessment may indicate that students are to have 35 minutes to work on the reading comprehension section of the assessment. If a teacher allows students to work for more than 35 minutes or less than 35 minutes, the standards for the test have been violated and the scores are invalidated. Adhering to the specific instructions provided for standardized tests is critical because of the statistical basis of the reported scores.

While standardized tests can be either *criterion-referenced* or *norm-referenced*, most of the widely used assessments are norm-referenced. General achievement tests, such as the Metropolitan Achievement Test or the Stanford Achievement Test, contain several different sections that assess students' literacy skills. The MAT-8, for example, measures emergent literacy, phonics, spelling, vocabulary, and comprehension and also recommends lexiles for each student (Pearson, 2013a). Similarly, the SAT-10 assesses spelling, language, sounds and letters, and reading comprehension and also provides lexile information for each student (Pearson, 2013b). Many school districts administer a general achievement test in most grade levels near the end of each school year.

In additional to general achievement tests, there are other standardized assessments that relate specifically to literacy skills. These assessments tend to be administered by reading specialists who are working with at-risk students or students who have been identified as having reading difficulties.

Interpreting Standard Scores

Appropriately interpreting the scores obtained from standardized assessments is critical if the information is to be useful. All standardized assessment scores begin with the *raw score*, or the number of items that were correctly answered on the assessment. The raw score is utilized to calculate other scores, called *derived scores*. Examples of commonly used derived scores are *stanines, percentiles,* and *grade-equivalent scores*. Standard scores used in educational assessments are based on the normal distribution (bell curve), often with a mean of 100 and a *standard deviation* of 15. For example, an IQ score of 130 is two standard deviations above the mean. The standard deviation is a number that indicates the magnitude of the spread of the scores. A low standard deviation indicates a smaller range of scores while a higher deviation indicates a large range of scores.

Stanines ("standard nines") are standard scores that range from 1 to 9, with a mean of 5 and a standard deviation of 2, with the bell curve divided into 9 segments. In general, when interpreting stanines, stanines 1–3 represent below level achievement, 4–6 represent average achievement, and 7–9 represent above-average achievement.

Percentiles are standard scores that range from 1 to 99, with a mean of 50. The percentile represents the percentage of students in the norming sample who scored at or below that score. For example, a percentile of 37 means that 37 percent of the students in the norming sample scored at or below that score. Stated another way, a student who earned a percentile of 73 would have scored at the same level or higher than 73 percent of the students in the norming sample. In general, most achievement tests provide national percentiles, and state-developed achievement tests may report both state and national percentiles.

Grade-equivalent (GE) scores are often reported on educational achievement tests and similar assessments. A GE of 4.6 would be read as "fourth grade, sixth month." A grade-equivalent score compares the student's achievement to that of students at other grade levels, on the same material. A GE score of 7.3, for example, means that the student scored the same as the average student in the third month of seventh grade on the material that was assessed. It does *not* mean that the student is doing seventh-grade-level work.

Uses of Standardized Literacy Assessments

Standardized assessments, including standardized literacy assessments, are not particularly useful for classroom teachers on a day-to-day basis. The results of standardized assessments do not provide the type of information that can be used to inform instruction. Instead, standardized assessments are often used to:

- Compare groups of 25 or more students with other groups of more than 25 students, such as classes compared to classes or schools compared to other schools
- Obtain an overall idea of a student's achievement in terms of his or her ranking compared with other students of the same age/grade

Care needs to be taken in order to effectively utilize standardized assessment data. While most teachers understand percentiles, fewer of them really understand stanines and grade-equivalent scores. Parents and care-givers often have no background in interpreting the results of standardized assessments and often have incorrect ideas about what the standard scores mean.

One standard score that causes much confusion is the *grade-equivalent score* (GE), often reported for standardized assessments. Many parents believe the GE score means that their students are actually able to do school work at that level. For example, when a fourth-grade student receives a GE of 8.6 on a standardized reading assessment, parents may interpret this to mean that the student can read text written on an eighth-grade level. Because the GE score is so confusing to both teachers and parents, several professional organizations, including the International Reading Association and the National Council of Teachers of English, recommend that GE scores should not be used at all.

Assessing Quality of Standardized Literacy Assessments

Selecting high-quality standardized literacy assessments is usually the task of the school administration or committees of teachers charged with reviewing available assessments and selecting the best one for their schools. All teachers should be aware of the qualities of standardized literacy assessments so that they can actively participate in assessment selection and can provide feedback regarding the assessments selected for use by the school administration.

When selecting high-quality, standardized literacy assessments, the following criteria should be considered:

- **Match with the curriculum**
  A standardized assessment that does not align closely with the school's literacy curriculum is virtually worthless. The assessment cannot provide data related to overall student achievement if it does not measure what the students have actually been taught.
- **Match with the student population**
  There should be a match between the norming population upon which the assessment was standardized and the school population. For example, if the norming sample was comprised of 100 elementary students in rural Montana, it is unlikely that this norming population will provide data that will match a school population from an urban district in inner-city Pittsburgh.
- **Philosophy of literacy instruction**
  The assessment should match the philosophy of literacy learning that is held by the teachers in the school. Many standardized assessments treat literacy as a set of isolated skills and assess these skills in a multiple-choice format. If the school's philosophy is that literacy learning occurs best by using integrated curricula and authentic literacy activities, there is a mismatch between what is measured by the assessment and what the students are taught to do in the classroom. Teachers must consider what is measured by the assessment and determine whether or not the data obtained from the measured skills are an adequate or accurate picture of the students' literacy learning.

Common Standardized Literacy Assessments

There are literally hundreds of standardized literacy assessments available for use with K-12 students. Some of the assessments that are commonly found in classrooms include the following:

SAILS   Standardized Assessment of Information Literacy Skills

SAILS is a multiple-choice test that assesses information literacy skills for students in Gr. K-12.

GORT-IV   Gray Oral Reading Test 4th Edition

The GORT assesses a student's ability to read orally. Scores are given for reading rate, accuracy, fluency, and comprehension.

GSRT   Gray Silent Reading Tests

This assessment contains developmentally sequenced reading passages with five multiple-choice questions for each passage. The assessment provides information related to students' reading comprehension and is appropriate for ages 7 through 25.

GDRT-2   Gray Diagnostic Reading Tests 2nd Edition

This assessment is used to assess students who have difficulty reading continuous print. It provides a diagnostic evaluation of specific abilities related to reading, including letter/word identification, phonetic analysis, reading vocabulary, and meaningful reading. It is appropriate for students aged 6 to 14.

Woodcock Reading Mastery Tests

Assesses students, age 4 through adult, on phonological awareness, letter and word identification, oral reading, word attack, word comprehension, and passage comprehension. This assessment is administered individually.

Gates-MacGinitie Reading Tests

The Gates-MacGinitie reading tests are group-administered tests developed for students in grades K through adult. It is a diagnostic assessment designed for screening, diagnosis, or progress monitoring.

WRAT 4: Wide Range Achievement Test 4th Edition

The WRAT4 measures basic skills, including reading, spelling, and math computation, for individuals aged 5 through 94 years. It is administered individually.

Chapter Activities

1. During April of Grade 3, Meghan earned these scores on the national standardized achievement test administered by her school:

Subtest	Percentile	Stanine
Reading vocabulary	44	5
Reading comprehension	81	7
Total reading	63	6
Math concepts	92	8
Math computation	90	8
Total math	93	8
Language usage	40	4
Spelling	35	4
Social studies	42	5
Science	30	4

Answer these questions about Meghan's achievement:

a. What is one statement (fact) you can make about Meghan's achievement? Support your response with data from the chart.

b. If you were going to interpret Meghan's achievement for her parents, what would you say? Support your response using data from the chart.

c. What is one inference you can make from the data in the chart? (Something you think might be true based on the data, which will need more assessment to substantiate.) Support your response using data from the chart.

2. Students in a second-grade class earned the following scores when they completed the state-required standardized achievement test.

Student	Listening Comprehension				Vocabulary				Reading Comprehension			
	RS	PR	ST	GE	RS	PR	ST	GE	RS	PR	ST	GE
Mariah	15	36	4	2.1	20	80	7	3.6	20	62	6	3.4
Zachariah	28	90	8	4.7	25	99	9	5.2	38	96	9	5.7
Tomas	5	10	2	1.4	7	27	4	2.9	7	18	3	1.6

Answer these questions about the students listed in the chart:

a. If these scores are representative of the class of 30 students, what is one statement that you can make about the overall achievement of the class? Use data from the chart to support your response.

b. How would you explain Zachariah's listening comprehension scores to his parents?

c. Based on these test results, should you provide Mariah with a third-grade text to read independently during sustained silent reading (SSR)? Why or why not?

d. Identify one student about whom you have questions. List two questions you have about his or her performance. What might you do next to gather that information?

References

Pearson. (2013a). *Metropolitan Achievement Tests, Eight Edition*. Retrieved from: http://www
    .pearsonassessments.com/HAIWEB/Cultures/en-us/Productdetail.htm?Pid=E164C.
Pearson (2013b). *Stanford Achievement Tests, Tenth Edition*. Retrieved from: https://www
    .pearsonassessments.com/haiweb/cultures/en-us/productdetail.htm?pid=SAT10C.

CHAPTER 5

Informal Literacy Assessments: Emergent Literacy

Assessing Emergent Literacy

Assessing literacy development at the emergent literacy stage is critical, as students who fall behind during preschool and kindergarten are much more likely to struggle with literacy throughout elementary school and beyond. At the emergent literacy level, teachers may assess students' storybook reading, concepts about print, alphabet knowledge, phonological and phonemic awareness, and knowledge of letter/sound correspondences.

This chapter provides informal assessments designed to be used by classroom teachers in order to assess their students' emergent literacy development.

Assessments included in this chapter are as follows:

Assessment 5.1

Storybook-Reading Classification Assessment

Background

One of the first indications that a child is acquiring early literacy skills is when she picks up favorite storybooks and begins to "read" them on her own. The Classification Scheme for Emergent Reading of Favorite Storybooks is an assessment based on the emergent literacy research conducted by Elizabeth Sulzby (Valencia & Sulzby, 1991). Students will move through Sulzby's eleven levels, sometimes backtracking before moving forward and moving at different rates.

Grade Levels:	PK–1
Materials Needed:	Child-selected storybook
	Storybook-Reading Record Sheet
Data Generated:	Identifies the student's stage on the Sulzby Classification Scheme for Emergent Reading of Favorite Storybooks
Data Usage:	Use for periodic assessments to determine development of emergent literacy concepts and to inform instruction related to emergent literacy
Directions:	Teacher asks student to select a book to read aloud.
	As the student reads, teacher observes and identifies the student's level on the Sulzby Classification Scheme for Emergent Reading of Favorite Storybooks. Books should be story books that have a plot—not books that are patterned, which students can memorize verbatim. The child should be the one to hold the book and to turn the pages.
	Teacher completes the Storybook-Reading Record Sheet.

Reference

Sulzby, E. & Rockafellow, B. (2001). *Sulzby Classification Scheme Instructional Profiles.* Retrieved from: http://firstclass.msvl.k12.wa.us/~literacy/FOV1-000181DB/ FOV100017B9B/ FOV000192DF/Sulzby%20Classification%20Scheme.Article.pdf?FCItemID=S0081C5CB&Plugin= Metro.

Sulzby Storybook-Reading Classification Levels

Level	Typical Grades	Description
Levels 1–2		**Story is not formed; "reading" based on pictures.**
1	PK	Student comments about and labels illustrations.
2	PK	Student follows action as shown in the illustrations.
Levels 3–4		**Story is formed; "reading" is based on pictures.** **Sounds like oral language, not written language.**
3	PK	Student demonstrates basic storytelling with a beginning, middle, end.
4	PK	Student puts together a more well-formed story.
Levels 5–7		**Story is formed; not watching print.** **Reading is governed by the pictures.** **Sounds like story language.**
5	PK	Student uses mixture of reading and storytelling.
6	PK–1	Student tells a story similar to the original story and uses few self-corrections.
7	PK–1	Student tells a story that sounds very similar to the original.
Levels 8–11		**Story is formed.** **Reading is governed by print.**
8	Early 1st	Story is both print governed and print based. Student might refuse to read because he or she "can't read."
9	Middle 1st	Story is print governed; student is looking at print.
10	Middle 1st	Story is print governed; student looks at print and reads holistically with imbalanced strategies.
11	Late 1st	Student shows conventional reading behaviors with familiar books.

Storybook Reading Record Sheet

Student: _____

Date	Book	Level	Notes

Instructional Strategy Notes:

Assessment 5.2

Concepts About Print Assessment

Background

As children have authentic experiences with literacy, such as being read to by parents or teachers, they begin to develop ideas about how books work and how print is read. We call these understandings *concepts about print*. Concepts about print that students develop include concept of letter, concept of word, understanding that the print contains the meaning—not the pictures, book-handling and book orientation, directionality, return sweep, one-to-one correspondence, and knowledge of simple punctuation (i.e., period, question mark.)

The label *concepts about print* was first developed by Marie Clay, who developed a concept about print assessment utilizing several specific books. Since then, similar assessments have been developed that can be used with any book.

Grade Levels:	PK–K
Materials Needed:	Children's storybook (to be read by the teacher) that has pictures, a good storyline, and multiple lines of print on each page.
	Concepts About Print Assessment Record Sheet
	Writing implement
	Two colored index cards or 3 × 5 paper rectangles
Data Generated:	List of concepts about print that have and have not been mastered by the student
Data Usage:	Data can be compared over time to show development of concepts about print.
	Data can be used to inform instruction.
Directions:	Teacher works one-to-one with a student.
	Teacher reads book to student.
	As the assessment proceeds, teacher makes notes on the record sheet, adding details immediately after the assessment ends.

Reference

Clay, M.M. (2000). *Concepts About Print: What Have Children Learned About Printed Language?* Portsmouth, NH: Heinemann.

Concepts About Print Assessment Record Sheet

Name:_____ Date:_____Age: _____

Book:_____ Book Level:_____

Book Handling and Orientation

Hand the student the book, spine facing the child.

Direction to Student	Student Is Successful	Student Is Unsuccessful
Show me the front of the book.		
Show me the back of the book.		
Show me the title of the book.		
I am going to read this book to you. Show me where the story begins. (first page)		

Meaning Is in the Print Not Pictures

Open the book to the first page of the story.

Direction to Student	Student Is Successful	Student Is Unsuccessful
Point to the words on the page.		
Point to the picture on the page.		

Directionality

Stay on the first page of the story.

Direction to Student	Student Is Successful	Student Is Unsuccessful
Point to where I should start reading the story. (first word)		
Where do I go after that? (left-to-right, next word)		

Read the first page of the story to the student.

Direction to Student	Student Is Successful	Student Is Unsuccessful
Now that I have read this page, where do I read next? (page turn to next page)		

With the book open to a two-page spread, read the left page.

Point to the last word on the left page and ask:

Direction to Student	Student Is Successful	Student Is Unsuccessful
Where do I read next?		

Concept of Word and Concept of Letter

Give the student two index cards or pieces of colored paper. Demonstrate how to slide them together and apart to highlight something in-between the two cards.

Direction to Student	Student Is Successful	Student Is Unsuccessful
Show me one letter.		
Show me one word.		
Show me the first letter in this word (point to 1 word)		
Show me the last letter in this word (point to 1 word)		

Return Sweep

Turn to a page that has at least two lines of text on it. Read the first line of text, tracking with your finger as you move along the line. Keep your finger at the end of the first line.

Direction to Student	Student Is Successful	Student Is Unsuccessful
Where do I go after this to keep reading?		

One-to-One Correspondence (Text Matching)

Turn to a new page in the book.

Direction to Student	Student Is Successful	Student Is Unsuccessful
As I read this page to you, I want you to point to each word as I say it.		

Simple Punctuation

Read a page of text that has a period and/or a question mark on it. Use the index cards or paper squares to isolate the period or question mark.

Direction to Student	Student Is Successful	Student Is Unsuccessful
Period: *Do you know what this is called?*		
Period: *Do you know what it tells a reader?*		
Question Mark: *Do you know what this is called?*		
Question Mark: *Do you know what it tells a reader?*		

NOTES:

Score Summary

Book Handling and Orientation	_____/4
Meaning in Print not Pictures	_____/2
Directionality	_____/4
Concept of Letter/Concept of Word	_____/4
Return Sweep	_____/1
One-to-One Correspondence (Text Matching)	_____/1
Simple Punctuation: Period	_____/2
Simple Punctuation: Question Mark	_____/2
Total:	_____/20

Benchmarks: Beginning of Kindergarten: 0

Mid-year of Kindergarten: 10

End of Kindergarten   20

Alphabet Knowledge Assessment

Background

Alphabet knowledge is considered to be a predictor of future reading success. Determining which students cannot identify the letters of the alphabet allows the teacher to pay particular attention to those students during emergent literacy development activities in the classroom and to provide additional authentic experiences to help these students learn to identify more letters.

Some alphabet knowledge assessments, such as the one included in the DIBELS assessments, are timed. These assessments use benchmarks regarding the number of letters that students should be able to identify within one minute, according to their age/grade level. This alphabet knowledge assessment is *not* timed. It is designed to provide information that will inform instruction and allow the teacher to identify students who will benefit from more authentic literacy experiences with engaging texts to build their alphabet knowledge.

Grade Levels:	PK–K
Materials Needed:	Student Letter Sheet
	Alphabet Knowledge Assessment Record Sheet
	Alphabet Knowledge Developmental Record
	Writing implement
	Blank sheet of paper or ruler
Data Generated:	Provides list of letters that students can identify (capital and lower case)
Data Usage:	Can be used to track development (recommended: 3 times/year)
	Used to identify students who need additional authentic emergent literacy experiences
	Informs instruction in alphabet knowledge
Directions:	The teacher points to each letter on the student letter sheet as the student says the name of the letter. (It is often helpful to use a blank sheet of paper or a ruler placed below the row of letters that are being identified.) The teacher notes if the student correctly named the letter, gave the sound for the letter, or gave a word that begins with the letter. This assessment is ***untimed***.

Student Letter Sheet

O U H Q M E

B W L R V F

C X S I A Y

K D Z G N T

J P

u   k   t   f   h   a   l

e   s   g   w   y   m   r

x   b   z   v   n   c   i

o   d   p   j   q

Alphabet Knowledge Assessment Record Sheet

Name:_____   Date:_____

Grade:_____   Age:_____

N = Letter Name   S = Letter Sound   W = Word   I = Incorrect

	N	S	W	I		N	S	W	I		N	S	W	I
O					V					Z				
U					F					G				
H					C					N				
Q					X					T				
M					S					J				
E					I					P				
B					A					Capital Letters				
W					Y					N ____/26				
L					K					S ____/26				
R					D					W ____/26				

	N	S	W	I		N	S	W	I		N	S	W	I
u					w					i				
k					y					o				
t					m					d				
f					r					p				
h					x					j				
a					b					q				
l					z					Lowercase Letters				
e					v					N ____/26				
s					n					S ____/26				
g					c					W ____/26				

Notes:

Alphabet Knowledge Development Record

Name:_____   Grade: _____

Capital Letters

N = Letter Name   S = Letter Sound   W = Word   I = Incorrect

September	N	S	W	I	January	N	S	W	I	April	N	S	W	I
O					O					O				
U					U					U				
H					H					H				
Q					Q					Q				
M					M					M				
E					E					E				
B					B					B				
W					W					W				
L					L					L				
R					R					R				
V					V					V				
F					F					F				
C					C					C				
X					X					X				
S					S					S				
I					I					I				
A					A					A				
Y					Y					Y				
K					K					K				
D					D					D				
C					C					C				
G					G					G				
N					N					N				
T					T					T				
J					J					J				
P					P					P				

Comments:

Lower-Case Letters

N = Letter Name   S = Letter Sound   W = Word   I = Incorrect

	September					January					April			
	N	S	W	I		N	S	W	I		N	S	W	I
u					u					u				
k					k					k				
t					t					t				
f					f					f				
h					h					h				
a					a					a				
l					l					l				
e					e					e				
s					s					s				
g					g					g				
w					w					w				
y					y					y				
m					m					m				
r					r					r				
x					x					x				
b					b					b				
z					z					z				
v					v					v				
n					n					n				
c					c					c				
i					i					i				
o					o					o				
d					d					d				
p					p					p				
j					j					j				
q					q					q				

Comments:

Assessment 5.4

Phonological Awareness Assessment

Background

Phonological awareness is the ability to identify similarities and differences among sounds, including differences between words, rhyming, and alliteration. Phonological awareness can also be used as a predictor of reading success through grade two (Hogan, Catts & Little, 2005).

Grade Levels:	PK–K
Materials Needed:	Phonological Awareness Assessment
	Writing implement
Data Generated:	Results identify student's ability to identify words that rhyme, to generate rhyming words, and to identify and generate alliteration.
Data Usage:	Students who struggle with phonological awareness are more likely to have difficulty with reading development. This assessment can be used to identify students who are in need of additional authentic literacy experiences to support their language awareness.
Directions:	Assessment is administered one-to-one in a quiet environment.
	Teacher should sit next to or behind the student so that the student cannot see the teacher's mouth when the words are being read.

Reference

Hogan, T., Catts, H. W. & Little, T.D. (2005). *The Relationship Between Phonological Awareness and Reading: Implications for the Assessment of Phonological Awareness*. Special Education and Communication Disorders Faculty Publications. Paper 14. Retrieved from: http://digitalcommons.unl.edu/specedfacpub/14.

Phonological Awareness Assessment

Student:_____   Date:_____

Age:_____   Grade:_____

Discriminating Between Similar Words

Be sure that the student understands the words "same" and "different." Give the student a few examples if needed before beginning the assessment. Examples to use: like/like, monkey/kitten

Administrator: *I am going to say two words. If the words are the same, I want you to say, "Same." If the words are different, I want you to say, "Different." Are these words the same or different?*

Prompts	Correct Response	Correct	Incorrect
listen cold	different		
apple apple	same		
pickle pickle	same		
turn burn	different		
seed steed	different		
runny runny	same		
threw blew	different		
snore snow	different		
going growing	different		
nose nose	same		

Totals: ___/10   ___/10

Identifying Rhyming Words

Be sure the student understands what "rhyming" means. Explain that rhyming words sound the same in the middle and at the end, and give several examples, such as "cat" and "hat" and "sit" and "fit." Then give the student an example of words that do not rhyme, such as "cat" and "swim." When you are certain that the student understands what rhyming is, start the assessment.

Administrator: *I am going to say two words. Say "yes" if they rhyme and say "no" if they do not rhyme.*

Prompts	Correct Response	Correct	Incorrect
Do *run* and *fun* rhyme?	yes		
Do *sigh* and *fly* rhyme?	yes		
Do *cap* and *swim* rhyme?	no		
Do *kitten* and *mitten* rhyme?	yes		
Do *bog* and *sag* rhyme?	no		
Do *tin* and *bit* rhyme?	no		
Do *more* and *snore* rhyme?	yes		
Do *tug* and *mug* rhyme?	yes		
Do *met* and *set* rhyme?	yes		
Do *mister* and *mighty* rhyme?	no		

Totals: ____/10 ____/10

Producing Rhymes

Administrator: *Instead of telling me whether two words rhyme, I am going to tell you one word and I want you to tell me a word that rhymes with the word I say. For example, if I say, "Run," you could say, "Fun." Let's try a few for practice...*

Use these words for practice: cat . . ..   hit . . .

If the student needs additional practice, add a few more words until you are sure the student understands the object of the activity. (Note: Both real words and nonsense words count as correct as long as they rhyme with the given word.) Record the word the student says in the "student's response" column.

Prompts	Student's Response	Correct	Incorrect
What is a word that rhymes with "hog"?			
What is a word that rhymes with "mitt"?			
What is a word that rhymes with "run"?			
What is a word that rhymes with "say"?			
What is a word that rhymes with "flea"?			
What is a word that rhymes with "go"?			
What is a word that rhymes with "head"?			
What is a word that rhymes with "wish"?			
What is a word that rhymes with "chip"?			
What is a word that rhymes with "hand"?			

Totals: ____/10 ____/10

Creating Alliteration

Administrator: *I am going to make a tongue twister by saying some words that all start with the same sound. Here is an example: ten tiny toads. Here is another example: Peter planted posies. I am going to give you a word, and I want you to make it into a tongue twister. For example, if I say, "Lisa," you could say, "Lisa loved lemons." Are you ready to give it a try?*

As soon as you are sure the student understands the task, begin the assessment.

Prompts	Student Response	Correct	Incorrect
Make a tongue twister that starts with "Bob."			
Make a tongue twister that starts with "ten."			
Make a tongue twister that starts with "little."			
Make a tongue twister that starts with "red."			
Make a tongue twister that starts with "girls."			

Totals: ____ /5   ____ /5

Phonological Awareness Assessment Score Summary

Task	Number of Correct Response	Percentage Correct
Word Discrimination	/10	
Identifying Rhyming Words	/10	
Producing Rhymes	/10	
Creating Alliteration	/5	

NOTES:

Phonemic Awareness Assessment

Background

Phonemic awareness is the ability to manipulate sounds in words. Students with good phonemic awareness are able to isolate phonemes in words, add and delete phonemes from words, substitute phonemes in words, identify words that contain the same phoneme, segment words into their phonemic components, and blend phonemes into words. Phonemic awareness is a skill that is important for students who are learning to read alphabetic-based languages. Research has shown that students who have difficulty with phonemic awareness tasks often have difficulty with other reading development.

This assessment should be used with students who are not demonstrating the ability to manipulate sounds in literacy activities or in their daily writing.

Grade Levels:	PK–1
Materials Needed:	Phonemic Awareness Assessment
	Writing implement
Data Generated:	Assessment results will indicate whether students are skilled in manipulating language sounds.
Data Usage:	Students who perform poorly on phonemic awareness tasks are at risk for future reading difficulties. Data can be used to identify students who will benefit from additional authentic literacy experiences related to the sounds of language.
Directions:	Assessment is administered one-to-one in a quiet environment.
	Teacher should sit next to or behind the student so that the student cannot see the teacher's mouth when the words are being read.

Reference

Hoover, W.A. (2002). The Importance of Phonemic Awareness in Learning to Read. *SEDL Letter,* *XIV*(3). Retrieved from: http://www.sedl.org/pubs/sedl-letter/v14n03/3.html

Phonemic Awareness Assessment

Student:_____ Date:_____ Age/Grade:_____

Phoneme Isolation

Initial Phoneme Isolation

Administrator: *Say the sound you hear at the beginning of the word . . .*

Word	Correct Response	Correct	Incorrect
cap	/k/		
toy	/t/		
piano	/p/		
mouse	/m/		
song	/s/		

Totals: _____/5   _____/5

Final Phoneme Isolation

Administrator: *Say the sound you hear at the end of the word . . .*

Word	Correct Response	Correct	Incorrect
rat	/t/		
Sad	/d/		
bear	/r/		
man	/n/		
bell	/l/		

Totals: _____/5   _____/5

Phoneme Deletion

Administrator: *If I take the /b/ sound away from the beginning of the word "boy," I would have /oy/. I want you to take away the beginning sound of each of the words I say and tell me what sounds are left.*

Prompt	Correct Response	Correct	Incorrect
If I take away the /m/ from money, what sounds are left?	/oney/		
If I take away the /g/ from goat, what sounds are left?	/oat/		
If I take away the /l/ from lake, what sounds are left?	/ake/		
If I take away the /w/ from way what sounds are left?	/ay/		
If I take away the /r/ from ring, what sounds are left?	/ing/		

Totals: _____/5   _____/5

Phoneme Addition

Administrator: *If I have the word "at" and I add the sound /s/ to the beginning of it, I would have the word "sat." I want you to add the sounds I tell you to the beginning of the words I say.*

Prompt	Correct Response	Correct	Incorrect
If I add the sound /p/ to the beginning of the word 'in' what word do I have?	pin		
If I add the sound /m/ to the beginning of the word "oat," what word do I have?	moat		
If I add the sound /t/ to the beginning of the word "am," what word do I have?	tam		
If I add the sound /w/ to the beginning of the word "ill," what word do I have?	will		
If I add the sound /h/ to the beginning of the word 'ick," what word do I have?	hick		

Totals: _____/5   _____/5

Phoneme Categorization

Administrator: *I am going to say some words. I want you to tell me which word does not belong with the others in the group.* Note: Teacher should circle the word that the student says.

Prompts	Student's Response	Correct Response	Correct	Incorrect
pick, patch, big, pill		big		
mill, monkey, mat, nice		nice		
sign, tummy, silly, sad		tummy		
big, pumpkin, banging, bird		pumpkin		
little, hinge, happy, hello		little		

Totals: _____/5 _____/5

Phoneme Substitution

Administrator: *I am going to say a word and then change it. For example, if I say the word "bite" and I take away the /b/ and put on the sound /k/, I would have the word "kite."*

Prompt	Correct Response	Correct	Incorrect
If I take the /m/ away from "mate" and add the sound /l/, what word do I have?	late		
If I take the /p/ away from "ping" and add the sound /st/, what word do I have?	sting		
If I take the /wh/ away from "white" and add the sound /qu/, what word do I have?	quite		
If I take the /b/ away from "bill" and add the sound /p/, what word do I have?	pill		
If I take the /h/ away from "happy" and add the sound /n/, what word do I have?	nappy		

Totals: _____/5 _____/5

Phoneme Segmentation

Administrator: *I am going to say a word, and I want you to tell me what sounds you hear in the word. For example, if I said the word "sit," you would say /s/ /i/ /t/*

Prompt	Student's Response	Correct Response	Correct	Incorrect
tag		/t/ /a/ /g/		
hill		/h/ /i/ /l/		
seep		/s/ /e/ /p/		
red		/r/ /e/ /d/		
not		/n/ /o/ /t/		
go		/g/ /o/		
luck		/l/ /u/ /k/		
pup		/p/ /u/ /p/		
goose		/g/ /oo/ /s/		
hop		/h/ /o/ /p/		

Totals: _____/10   _____/10

Phoneme Blending

Administrator: *"I am going to say some sounds and I want you to put them together to make a word. For example, if I say, /d/ /o/ /g/, you would say, "Dog."*

Prompt	Student Response	Correct Response	Correct	Incorrect
/t/ /a/ /g/		Tag		
/h/ /i/ /m/		Him		
/r/ /o/ /p/		Rope		
/s/ /t/ /o/ /p/		Stop		
/f/ /i/ /sh/		Fish		

Totals: _____/5   _____/5

Phonemic Awareness Assessment Score Summary

Phonemic Awareness Skill	Number of Correct Response	Percentage Correct
Phoneme Isolation: Beginning	/5	
Phoneme Isolation: Ending	/5	
Phoneme Deletion	/5	
Phoneme Addition	/5	
Phoneme Categorization	/5	
Phoneme Substitution	/5	
Phoneme Segmentation	/10	
Phoneme Blending	/5	

TOTALS: _____/45 _____%

NOTES:

Assessing Phonemic Awareness Using Invented Spelling

Background

Using invented spelling helps strengthen students' understanding of the connections between sounds and written language. Since students should be writing daily, even at the emergent literacy stage, analyzing their writing provides data for the teacher without having to administer a separate phonemic awareness assessment. Students who are not demonstrating development in their invented spelling can be assessed further by using a specific phonemic awareness assessment, such as Assessment 5.5.

Grade Levels:	PK–1
Materials Needed:	Student writing samples or journal
Data Generated:	Assessment results will indicate whether students are skilled in segmenting and blending sounds into words.
Data Usage:	Data can be used to identify students who will benefit from additional authentic literacy experiences related to the sounds of language and who may benefit from more specific phonemic awareness assessment.
Directions:	Teacher uses the invented spelling analysis chart to determine a student's level of phonemic awareness.
	<u>Attempted Word Column</u>: The correct spelling of the word the student was trying to write
	<u>Number of Sounds Column</u>: The number of sounds in the word the student was trying to write
	<u>Student's Word Column</u>: The word as written by the student (invented spelling)
	<u>Number of Sounds Column</u>: The number of sounds that are represented in the word as written by the student
	<u>Similarities Column</u>: Put a check mark in the column(s) that represent the sounds the student included in the invented spelling.
Analysis:	Examine the similarities column to determine whether the student is demonstrating phonemic awareness of beginning, middle, and ending sounds.

Invented Spelling Analysis Chart for Assessing Phonemic Awareness

Student: _____ Date: _____ Age/Grade: _____

Attempted Word	Number of Sounds	Student's Word	Number of Sounds	Similarities		
				Beginning Consonant	Middle Vowel	Ending Consonant
Cake	3	cack	3	✓		✓

Assessment 5.7

Letter–Sound Correspondence Assessment

Background:	Reading researchers have found that students' knowledge of letters to be a strong predictor of future reading success. A strong understanding of letter–sound correspondences and patterns is also important for spelling development.
Grade Levels:	PK–1
Materials Needed:	Student Letter Sheet (Assessment 5.3)
	Letter–Sound Correspondence Record Sheet
	Alphabet Knowledge Developmental Record (Assessment 5.3)
	Writing implement
Data Generated:	Assessment results will provide teachers with a list of the letters (capital and lower case) for which the students can provide a corresponding sound.
Data Usage:	Assessment data can be used to chart students' development of alphabet knowledge over time. In addition, data can be used to identify students who will benefit from additional authentic literacy experiences that will support the learning of letter–sound correspondences.
Directions:	1. Use the Student Letter Sheet from Assessment 5.3. Ask the student to point to each letter and give the sound made by that letter. For vowels, accept either the long or short vowel sound as correct. For the letter *c*, the hard c sound (as in cat) is correct. For the letter *g*, the hard g sound (as in go) is correct.
	2. Note down the student's responses using the Letter–Sound Correspondence Assessment Record sheet, recording for each letter whether the student provides the letter name, letter sound, or a word for each letter.
	3. Track the student's results using the Alphabet Knowledge Developmental Record, which was included with Assessment 5.3. This record sheet will allow you to see at a glance whether the student can name each letter and give its sound.

Reference

Piasta, S. B. & Wagner, R. K. (2010). Developing Early Literacy Skills: A Meta-Analysis of Alphabet Learning and Instruction. *Reading Research Quarterly, 45*(1), 8-38.

Letter–Sound Correspondence Assessment Record Sheet

Name:_____ Date:_____

Grade:_____ Age:_____

N = Letter Name   S = Letter Sound   W = Word   I = Incorrect

	N	S	W	I		N	S	W	I		N	S	W	I
O					V					Z				
U					F					G				
H					C					N				
Q					X					T				
M					S					J				
E					I					P				
B					A									
W					Y					Capital Letters				
L					K					N _____/26				
R					D					S _____/26				
										W _____/26				

	N	S	W	I		N	S	W	I		N	S	W	I
u					w					i				
k					y					o				
t					m					d				
f					r					p				
h					x					j				
a					b									
l					z					Lower-Case Letters				
e					v					N _____/26				
s					n					S _____/26				
g					c					W _____/26				

Notes:

Assessing Letter–Sound Correspondence Using Invented Spelling

Background

Using invented spelling helps strengthen students' understanding of the connections between sounds and written language. Since students should be writing daily, even at the emergent literacy stage, analyzing their writing provides data for the teacher without having to administer a separate assessment to identify their knowledge of letter–sound correspondences.

Students who are not demonstrating development in their invented spelling can be assessed further by using a specific assessment of letter–sound correspondence, such as Assessment 5.7.

Grade Level:	PK–1
Materials Needed:	Student writing samples or journal
Data Generated:	Assessment results will indicate students' knowledge of common letter/sound correspondences.
Data Usage:	Data can be used to identify students who will benefit from additional authentic literacy experiences related to the sounds of language and who may benefit from more specific instruction and activities related to letter/sound correspondences.
Directions:	Teacher uses the invented spelling analysis chart to determine a student's current knowledge of letter/sound relationships.

Attempted Word Column: The correct spelling of the word the student was trying to write

Number of Sounds Column: The number of sounds in the word the student was trying to write

Student's Word Column: The word as written by the student (invented spelling)

Number of Sounds Column: The number of sounds that are correctly represented by the appropriate letter in the word as written by the student. Note: As long as the letter written does make the sound that is heard in the word, the word does not need to be spelled correctly. For example, if the student is writing the word *cake* and spells it *kak*, the sounds in the word have been correctly represented by an appropriate letter

Correspondences Column: List all the letters used correctly by the student in the invented spelling. In the *cake* example above, the student would get credit for knowing the sounds of the letters *a* and *k*. List the letters that the student used incorrectly in the *incorrect* column.

Analysis: When analyzing the student's work, remember this is an assessment for examining student's knowledge of basic letter/sound correspondences. It is not a spelling assessment but designed to assess the emergent writer's knowledge of the most typical sound/symbol correspondences. Look for knowledge of regular sounds.

Invented Spelling Analysis Chart for Assessing Letter/Sound Correspondence

Student: _____ Date: _____ Age/Grade: _____

Attempted Word	Number of Sounds	Student's Word	Number of Sounds	Correspondences	
				Correct	Incorrect
light	3	lete	3	l, t	e (long i)

Assessment 5.9

Yopp-Singer Test of Phoneme Segmentation

Background:

Grade Levels:	PK–1
Materials Needed:	Word list
	Answer key
	Writing implement
Data Generated:	This assessment will provide a score that will indicate the student's level of understanding of phoneme segmentation and phonemic awareness.
Data Usage:	Students whose scores indicate that they are lacking in phonemic awareness should be involved in activities that will build this awareness.
Directions:	This assessment is given orally; students should not see the words at any time during the assessment.
	The test is administered individually to one student at a time.
	The student's attempts to segment the words in the assessment are recorded on the line. If the student is correct, circle the number of that item on the record form.
	If the student is incorrect, give the correct response and go to the next word.
	The student's score is the number of words that were segmented correctly. The entire word must be correct for it to be counted as correct.

Reference

Yopp, H.K. (1995). A test for assessing phonemic awareness in young children. *The Reading Teacher, 49*, 20-29.

Yopp-Singer Test of Phoneme Segmentation

Administrator: *Today we're going to play a word game. I'm going to say a word and I want you to break the word apart. You are going to say the word slowly and then tell me each sound in the word in order. For example, if I say, "Old," you should say /o/-/l/-/d/.* (The administrator says the sound, not the letters.)

Do a few samples with the student: ride, go, man.

When you think the student understands the directions, continue with the assessment.

Student's name _____ Date _____

Score (number correct) _____/22

    Level of Phonemic Assessment: _____Phonemically Aware (17–22)
    (check one)   _____ Emerging Phonemic Awareness (7–16)
                                             _____ Lacks Appropriate Phonemic Awareness (0–6)

Circle those items that the student correctly segments; incorrect responses may be recorded on the blank line following the item.

1. dog _____
2. keep _____
3. fine _____
4. no _____
5. she _____
6. wave _____
7. grew _____
8. that _____
9. red _____
10. me _____
11. sat _____

12. lay _____
13. race _____
14. zoo _____
15. three _____
16. job _____
17. in _____
18. ice _____
19. at _____
20. top _____
21. by _____
22. do _____

Yopp-Singer Test of Phoneme Segmentation

Answer Key

1. dog _____/d/ - /o/ - /g/ _____
2. keep _____/k/ - /e/ - /p/ _____
3. fine _____/f/-/i/-/n/ _____
4. no _____/n/- /o/ _____
5. she _____/sh/- /e/ _____
6. wave _____/w/ - / a/ - /v/ _____
7. grew _____/g/- /r/- /oo/ _____
8. that _____/th/- /a/- /t/ _____
9. red _____/r/- /e/- /d/ _____
10. me _____/m/- /e/ _____
11. sat _____/s/ - /a/- /t/ _____

12. lay _____/l/-/a/ _____
13. race _____/r/- /a/- /s/ _____
14. zoo _____/z/ - /oo/ _____
15. three_____/th/- /r/ - /e/ _____
16. job _____/j/- /o/ - /b/ _____
17. in _____/i/ - /n/ _____
18. ice _____/i/-/s/ _____
19. at _____/a/- /t/ _____
20. top _____/t/- /o/- /p/ _____
21. by _____/b/-/i/ _____
22. do _____/d/- /oo/ _____

Scoring Guide:

Number Correct	Rating
17–22	Phonemically Aware
7–16	Emerging Phonemic Awareness
0–6	Lacks Appropriate Phonemic Awareness

Additional Emergent Literacy Assessments

In addition to informal assessments, there are numerous commercially prepared and distributed emergent literacy assessments. A few of the more commonly used ones include the following:

Emerging Literacy and Language Assessment (ELLA)

The ELLA assessment is designed for children ages 4–11, depending upon the subtest being used. It requires approximately 35–60 minutes for administration and is available only in English. Computerized scoring is not yet available. Designed to be a "comprehensive phonological assessment," the ELLA also is billed as the only test of emerging literacy and language with a Story Retell section. Scores generated include standard scores, percentile ranks, and age equivalents. It is both norm- and criterion referenced.

Wiig, E. & Secord, W. (2006). *ELLA: Emerging Literacy & Language Assessment*. Super Duper Publications.

The Bridge Assessment

The Bridge Assessment is a portfolio rating scale developed by the Wake County Schools Emergent Literacy Project in North Carolina. It is a comprehensive scale that assesses a minimum of three pieces of evidence (observation notes, work samples, pictures, dictation) for students in each of these areas: Foundations of Reading (Book Knowledge/Appreciation/Print Awareness/Story Comprehension), Foundations of Writing, Alphabet Knowledge, Phonological/Phonemic Awareness, and Oral Language. The entire assessment instrument is available on the website.

Website: http://www.med.unc.edu/ahs/clds/resources/early-childhood-resources-1/the-bridge-assessment.

Assessment of Literacy and Language

The *Assessment of Literacy and Language* (ALL) is an individually administered assessment for students in grades PK–1. The assessment administration takes one hour or less. Both norm-referenced and criterion-referenced scores are provided. ALL assesses listening comprehension, language comprehension, semantics, syntax, phonological awareness, alphabetic principle/phonics, and concepts about print.

Website: https://images.pearsonclinical.com/images/products/all/3906_All_TR_f_LoRes.pdf.

Emergent Literacy Resources

Books

Bear, D.R., et al. (2018). Words Their Way Letter and Picture Sorts for Emergent Spellers (3rd Edition). New York: Pearson. ISBN-13: 978-0134773674.

Fu, Danling, et al. (2019). *Translanguaging for Emergent Bilinguals: Inclusive Teaching in the Linguistically Diverse Classroom.* New York: Teachers College Press. ISBN-13: 978-0807761120.

Garcia, O. & Kleifgen, J.A. (2018). *Educating Emergent Bilinguals: Policies, Programs, and Practices for English Learners.* New York: Teachers College Press. ISBN-13: 978-0807758854.

Websites

Emergent Literacy Podcasts by the Florida Dept. of Education https://itunes.apple.com/us/itunes-u/emergent-literacy/id399607365

Using Shared Storybook Reading to Promote Emergent Literacy http://archive.brookespublishing.com/newsletters/downloads/11Tips.pdf

Concepts About Print Assessment https://studylib.net/doc/8911839/concepts-about-print-scale-assessment-for-child-observati...

Concepts About Print Checklist http://www.stannes.cheshire.sch.uk/serve_file/5121

Emergent Literacy Assessment and Instruction Matrix

Skill/Concept	Assessment	Development Activities
Book Handling	5.1	Read Alouds
Meaning in Print	5.1	Environmental Print Walk
		Environmental Print Collage
		Language Experience Approach
		Morning Message
Concept of Letter	5.2	Echo Reading/Pointing
Concept of Word		Counting Words
		Being the Words
		Traffic Lights
Directionality	5.2	Echo Reading/Pointing
		Jumbled Sentences
		Being the Words
		Green Means Go
Return Sweep	5.2	Big Books with Pointers/Shared Reading
		Echo Reading/Pointing
		Green Means Go
		Highlighter Sweep
1:1 Matching	5.2	Big Books with Pointers/Shared Reading
		Echo Reading/Pointing
		Being the Words
		Language Experience Approach
		Morning Message
Alphabet		
Knowledge	5.3	Daily Writing Journals
	5.7	Dough Alphabet/Pretzel Alphabet
	5.8	Alphabet Clothesline
		Alphabet Thief
		Alphabet Scavenger Hunt
		Food Labels Alphabet
		Letter Bingo
		Letter Concentration
		Fingerpainting Letters

Skill/Concept	Assessment	Development Activities
		Sandpaper Letters
		Letter Collages
		Letter Sorting
		Alphabet Books
Word		
Differentiation	5.4	Traffic Lights
Rhyming Words	5.4	Predictable Rhyming Books
		Poems and Fingerplays
Alliteration		
Production	5.4	Tongue Twisters
		Alliterative Books
Phoneme	5.5	Daily Writing Journals
Manipulation	5.6	Letter–Sound Matching Activities
	5.9	
Letter/Sound	5.7	Daily Writing Journals
Correspondences	5.8	Predictable Rhyming Books
		Letter–Sound Dominoes
		Letter–Sound Memory/Concentration Games
		Letter–Sound Bingo
		Alphabet Books (Personalized)

Chapter Activities

1. Use the Invented Spelling Analysis Chart from Assessment 5.6 to assess a student's writing sample to determine his or her phonemic awareness. When you have finished completing the chart, write a summary of your analysis of the data.

2. Use the Invented Spelling Analysis Chart from Assessment 5.8 to assess a student's writing sample to determine his or her knowledge of letter/sound correspondences. When you have finished completing the chart, write a summary of your analysis of the data.

3. Assume that you are teaching the student whose phonemic awareness and letter/sound correspondence assessments you completed for activities 2 and 3. Identify two activities you would use with this student in order to support his or her development of both phonemic awareness and letter/sound correspondences. Be specific with your activities; for example, if they would involve reading a book, identify the specific book. Identify which specific phonemic awareness skills or letters will be the focus of the activity.

4. Administer the Yopp-Singer Test of Phonemic Segmentation (5.9) to a child in grade 2 or younger. Assess the student's level of phonemic awareness using the data from the assessment. Suggest at least two activities that you would use with this student to help build his or her phonemic awareness. Provide a rationale for your choices.

Informal Literacy Assessments: Prior Knowledge, Interests, and Motivation

Importance of Prior Knowledge, Motivation, and Interests

Assessing prior knowledge prior to instruction is a critical step, regardless of the subject area, but is especially critical for literacy instruction. If students do not have prior knowledge that is sufficient and correct, comprehension will be negatively impacted. In addition, if this prior knowledge is not activated prior to instruction, students will be unable to utilize it to support comprehension.

Many students dislike reading and literacy activities usually because they find them to be difficult. In order to build students' motivation to read and write, it is important to be aware of their attitudes and to understand the subjects that interest them. To inform instruction, teachers can utilize interest and attitude assessments to assist them in engaging students in literacy-related activities.

This chapter provides informal assessments designed to be used by classroom teachers in order to assess their students' prior knowledge, interests, and attitudes related to literacy instruction.

Assessments included in this chapter are as follows:

Assessment 6.1	Assessing Prior Knowledge
Assessment 6.2	Primary Interest Assessment
Assessment 6.3	Intermediate Interest Assessment
Assessment 6.4	Primary Attitude Assessment
Assessment 6.5	Intermediate Attitude Assessment

Assessment 6.1

Assessing Prior Knowledge

Background

The level of students' prior knowledge about a topic has a major impact on reading comprehension, and on learning, in general. Teachers should consider the level of students' prior knowledge when planning all lessons. There are numerous ways to assess prior knowledge relatively quickly and easily; many of these assessments also serve to activate students' prior knowledge at the same time.

Grade Levels: All

Data Usage: When assessments indicate that students do not have adequate prior knowledge related to the subject of the lesson, time should be spent building prior knowledge before the lesson. In addition, if assessment identifies that students have incorrect or incomplete prior knowledge, this should also be addressed prior to instruction.

General

Prior Knowledge

Assessments:

1. Ask students brief questions that relate to important concepts and vocabulary included in the text.
   For example,
   Where is *Kentucky*?

   What is a *meteor*?

2. Ask students open-ended questions that relate to important concepts and vocabulary included in the text.
   For example, What do you think of when you hear the word *ocean?*

3. Develop brief multiple-choice or short-answer pretests that students will complete prior to reading the text or participating in the lesson.
   For example, An *aardvark* is a _____.
   a. a bird
   b. a mammal
   c. an insect
   d. a fish

4. Develop lists of concepts or ideas related to a text that is going to be read. Ask students to put a check next to the ones that would be most likely to be in the text.
   For example, We are going to be reading a book about the zoo. Which of these things do you think might be included in the book?

   _____ puppies   _____ alligators   _____ balloons   _____ lions

   _____ giraffes   _____ clowns   _____ zebras   _____ cages

5. For young children, you can show felt pieces on a felt board or pictures on cards that relate to the text. Ask students to sort the pieces or pictures into two groups according to whether or not they will be in the book.

   For example, We are going to be reading a book about going to the library. Which of these things do you think might be included in the book?

© photographer/Shutterstock.com

Additional Prior Knowledge Assessment/Activation Activities

- Picture Walk/Text Walk
- Predictogram
- Think-Pair-Share/Write-Pair-Share
- ABC Brainstorming
- Carousel Brainstorming
- Brainstorming-List-Group-Label
- KWL and Variations
- Semantic Impressions/Story Impressions
- Concept Maps
- Anticipation Guides
- Talking Drawings
- THIEVES

Interest Assessments

Background

To motivate students to engage with literacy-related activities and with a variety of texts, it is important to include materials and activities that appeal to the student's interests. An interest assessment will provide teachers with information related to students' interests so that appropriate materials and texts can be selected for each student.

Grade Levels:	K–3: Primary Interest Assessment
	4–6: Intermediate Interest Assessment
Materials Needed:	Primary or Intermediate Interest Assessment
	Writing implement
Data Generated:	Data will reveal information about students' interests.
Data Usage:	Identified interests can be used for planning literacy lessons, selecting texts for lessons and for addition to the classroom library, and for grouping students for cooperative activities.
Directions:	Students who are able to read independently may complete the assessment on their own. The teacher may administer the questionnaire as an interview for students who are unable to read it on their own.

Primary Interest Assessment

Name: _____ Date: _____ Grade: _____

1. **Which of the following activities do you like to do in your free time? Circle all the ones that you might choose.**

play video games	surf the Internet	ride my bicycle	read a book
play board games	visit my friends	play sports	watch TV
listen to music	make crafts	draw or paint	cook or bake

2. **If you were able to buy as many books as you want, what kinds of books would they be? Circle all the ones that you might choose.**

biographies	mysteries	funny books	jokes or riddles
cookbooks	animal books	poetry books	science books
science fiction	puzzle books	information books	true stories
fables/myths	graphic novels	comic books	how-to books

3. **Which of these books would you choose at a book fair? Circle as many of them as you would like.**

Junie B. Jones	*Captain Underpants*	*Magic Treehouse*	*Arthur*
Magic Schoolbus	*Curious George*	*First Grade Friends*	*Judy Moody*
Frog and Toad	*Ivy and Bean*	*Elephant & Piggie*	*Basil of Baker Street*
Henry & Mudge	*Dr. Seuss*	*Skippyjon Jones*	*Amelia Bedelia*
Spiderwick Chronicles	*Amber Brown*	*Froggy*	*Pete the Cat*
Don't Let the Pigeon	*Diary of A Wimpy Kid*	*Dork Diaries*	*Lunch Lady*
Time Warp Trio	*Pony Pals*	*Splat the Cat*	*Fancy Nancy*
Dragon Breath	*Goddess Girls*	*Mrs. Piggle Wiggle*	*Nate the Great*

4. **What is your favorite TV show?** _____

5. **What is your favorite movie?** _____

6. **What is your favorite sport?** _____

7. **What is your favorite animal?** _____

8. **What is your favorite holiday?** _____

9. **What is your favorite place to visit?** _____

10. **If you had a million dollars, what would you do with it?**

    _____

Intermediate Interest Assessment

Name: _____ Date: _____ Grade: _____

1. Which of the following activities do you like to do in your free time? Circle all the ones that you might choose.

play videogames	surf the Internet	skateboard/rollerblade	read a book
play board games	visit my friends	play sports	watch TV
listen to music	make crafts	draw or paint	cook or bake

2. If you were able to buy as many books as you want, what kinds of books would they be? Circle all the ones that you might choose.

biographies	mysteries	funny books	jokes or riddles
cookbooks	animal books	poetry books	science books
science fiction	puzzle books	information books	true stories
fables/myths	graphic novels	comic books	how-to books

3. Which of these books would you choose at a book fair? Circle as many of them as you would like.

Harry Potter	Percy Jackson	Diary of a Wimpy Kid
Spiderwick Chronicles	Chronicles of Narnia	Series of Unfortunate Events
Dragonbreath	Kane Chronicles	Sisters Grimm
39 Clues	Book of Ember	Mysterious Benedict Society
Fablehaven	Shadow Children	Wayside School
Magic Thief	Ramona	Peter & the Starcatchers
Enchanted	Andrew Lost	Fudge Series
Encyclopedia Brown	Heroes of Olympus	Wolves Chronicles
Anne of Green Gables	Hunger Games	Origami Yoda
Inkworld Series	Ascendance Trilogy	Twilight
Cirque du Freak	Gallagher Girls	Pretty Little Liars

4. What is your favorite TV show? _____

5. What is your favorite movie? _____

6. What is your favorite sport? _____

7. What is your favorite animal? _____

8. What is your favorite holiday? _____

9. What is your favorite place to visit? _____

10. If you had a million dollars, what would you do with it?

_____

Attitude Assessments

Background

Attitude assessments are used to provide the teacher with information related to a student's feelings and attitudes about reading and literacy tasks. Many students dislike reading and writing activities because they struggle with them. Others do not find them engaging. Identifying a student's attitudes about literacy tasks will assist the teacher in planning appropriate activities to engage all students.

Grade Levels:	K–3: Primary Attitude Assessment
	4–6: Intermediate Attitude Assessment
Materials Needed:	Primary or Intermediate Attitude Assessment
	Writing implement
Data Generated:	Data will reveal information about students' attitudes related to literacy tasks.
Data Usage:	Identifying students who have negative attitudes related to literacy activities will make teachers aware that they must select materials and activities that are designed to engage students and overcome their negative attitudes.
Directions:	Students who are able to read independently may complete the assessment on their own. The teacher may administer the questionnaire as an interview for students who are unable to read it on their own.

Primary Attitude Assessment

Color the face that describes how you feel about . . .

1. reading class in school   ☺   😐   ☹

2. getting a book for a birthday present   ☺   😐   ☹

3. writing an e-mail/letter to a friend   ☺   😐   ☹

4. writing a story   ☺   😐   ☹

5. spending your own money on a book   ☺   😐   ☹

6. having a magazine subscription   ☺   😐   ☹

7. listening to your teacher read a story aloud   ☺   😐   ☹

8. talking to a friend about a story you read   ☺   😐   ☹

9. drawing a picture about a story you read   ☺   😐   ☹

10. acting out a story you have read   ☺   😐   ☹

11. reading on a website   ☺   😐   ☹

12. going to the library to choose books yourself   ☺   😐   ☹

13. learning to read new words   ☺   😐   ☹

14. learning to spell new words   ☺   😐   ☹

15. writing in your writing journal   ☺   😐   ☹

Intermediate Attitude Assessment

Circle the word that best tells how you would feel in each of these situations.

1. Reading aloud during reading class	happy	sad	excited	angry
2. Selecting a book in the library	happy	sad	excited	angry
3. Reading information on a website	happy	sad	excited	angry
4. Writing a story on the computer	happy	sad	excited	angry
5. Writing a story with a pen or pencil	happy	sad	excited	angry
6. Reading a science book	happy	sad	excited	angry
7. Reading a history book	happy	sad	excited	angry
8. Learning the meanings of new words	happy	sad	excited	angry
9. Looking up words in a dictionary	happy	sad	excited	angry
10. Sharing my writing with a friend	happy	sad	excited	angry
11. Sharing my writing with the class	happy	sad	excited	angry
12. Editing my writing	happy	sad	excited	angry
13. Reading a book I chose myself	happy	sad	excited	angry
14. Reading a book assigned by the teacher	happy	sad	excited	angry
15. Drawing a picture about a story	happy	sad	excited	angry
16. Acting out a story	happy	sad	excited	angry
17. Writing a new ending to a story	happy	sad	excited	angry
18. Having a magazine subscription	happy	sad	excited	angry
19. Buying a book at the book fair	happy	sad	excited	angry
20. Making a video about a book	happy	sad	excited	angry

Additional Interest and Attitude Assessments

Garfield Reading Attitude Survey:
http://www.professorgarfield.org/parents_teachers/printables/pdfs/reading/readingsurvey.pdf

Easily Printable Copy with Scoring Sheet:
http://resources.corwin.com/sites/default/files/Compendium_17.pdf

Scholastic Reading Interest Survey:
http://www.scholastic.com/content/collateral_resources/pdf/s/SB1711%20Dec_3-5_ReadingInterest_
    LO1.pdf

Elementary Reading Attitude Survey:
https://schools.liberty.k12.ga.us/jwalts/reading%20materials/Elementary%20Reading%20
    Attitude%20Survey.pdf

Reading Attitudes Survey (Ages 5–12):

Denver Reading Attitude Survey (Ages 8–12):
https://nashtoolkit.weebly.com/attitudes-survey.html

Prior Knowledge, Interests, and Attitudes

Assessment and Instruction Matrix

Skill/Concept	Assessment	Activities/Ideas
Prior Knowledge	6.1	Predictogram
		Picture Walk/Text Walk
		Think-Pair-Share/Turn and Talk
		Text Sets
		Videos
		Jigsaw
		Brainstorming, List-Group-Label
		Carousel Brainstorming
Interests	6.2, 6.3	Sustained Silent Reading (SSR)
		Book Self-Selection
		Cooperative Learning
		Literature Circles
		Book Clubs
		Book Talks
		Jackdaws
		Teacher Read-Alouds
Attitudes	6.4, 6.5	Sustained Silent Reading (SSR)
		Book Self-Selection
		Cooperative Learning
		Literature Circles
		Work on Correct Level
		Provide Scaffolding
		Teacher Read-Alouds
		Reading Bingo

Chapter Activities

1. Analyze the completed interest inventory below. It is for Lizzie, who is a second-grade student. Assuming that Lizzie is reading on a second-grade level, identify five books that you might give her to read, based on this assessment. Provide the reading level for each book and list the source from which you obtained that reading level.

---

1. Which of the following activities do you like to do in your free time? Circle all the ones that you might choose.

play videogames	surf the Internet	ride my bicycle	read a book
play board games	visit my friends	play sports	watch TV
listen to music	make crafts	draw or paint	cook or bake

2. If you were able to buy as many books as you want, what kinds of books would they be? Circle all the ones that you might choose.

biographies	mysteries	funny books	jokes or riddles
cookbooks	animal books	poetry books	science books
science fiction	puzzle books	information books	true stories
fables/myths	graphic novel	comic books	how-to books

3. Which of these books would you choose at a book fair? Circle as many of them as you would like.

Junie B. Jones	Captain Underpants	Magic Treehouse	Arthur
Magic Schoolbus	Curious George	First Grade Friends	Judy Moody
Frog and Toad	Ivy and Bean	Elephant & Piggie	Splat the Cat
Henry & Mudge	Dr. Seuss	Skippyjon Jones	Amelia Bedelia
Boxcar Children	The Littles	Amber Brown	Froggy
Don't Let the Pigeon...	Diary of A Wimpy Kid	Dork Diaries	Lunch Lady
Berenstain Bears	Time Warp Trio	Pony Pals	

4. What is your favorite TV show? _hows_

5. What is your favorite movie? _skate moves_

6. What is your favorite sport? _Back it Ball_

7. What is your favorite animal? _Cats and Jag and fishs_

8. What is your favorite holiday? _Holowen_

9. What is your favorite place to visit? _Lah Hoseu_

10. If you had a million dollars, what would you do with it?

biu a car

2. Analyze the completed attitude inventory below. It is for Braden, who is a third-grade student. Summarize what this assessment tells you about Braden's attitude toward literacy activities. If you were his reading teacher, what are two activities you might try with Braden to improve his attitude? Provide a rationale for your ideas.

Primary Attitude Assessment

Color the face that describes how you feel about...

1.	reading class in school	😊	😐	☹️
2.	getting a book for a birthday present	😊	😐	☹️
3.	writing a letter to a friend	😊	😐	☹️
4.	writing a story	😊	😐	☹️
5.	spending your own money on a book	😊	😐	☹️
6.	having a magazine subscription	😊	😐	☹️
7.	listening to your teacher read a story aloud	😊	😐	☹️
8.	talking to a friend about a story you read	😊	😐	☹️
9.	drawing a picture about a story you read	😊	😐	☹️
10.	acting out a story you have read	😊	😐	☹️
11.	writing a poem	😊	😐	☹️
12.	going to the library to choose books yourself	😊	😐	☹️
13.	learning to read new words	😊	😐	☹️
14.	learning to spell new words	😊	😐	☹️
15.	writing in your writing journal	😊	😐	☹️

Informal Literacy Assessments: Word Skills

Assessing Word Knowledge

When determining a student's word-related knowledge, it is often useful to begin with an assessment of the words the student can identify by sight. In addition, teachers should assess the student's stage of word identification, to determine the developmental level at which the student is currently operating when attacking unknown words. This information is invaluable when planning instruction. Finally, it is useful to determine the strategies that a student currently uses when trying to identify unknown words, so that instruction in alternative strategies can be implemented.

This chapter includes two assessments that will provide teachers with information related to students' word identification strategies and knowledge of sight words.

Assessment 7.1   Sight Word Assessment

Assessment 7.2   Greene's Informal Word Analysis Inventory

Assessment 7.1

Sight Words Assessment

Background

In order for students to develop as fluent readers, it is necessary for them to acquire the ability to identify words quickly. Sight words play an important role in this development. Beginning readers have a limited sight word vocabulary. This vocabulary continues to develop until, by the time readers have reached the expert stage, almost all words are read as sight words.

Although many teachers have students practice sight words by reading them from flashcards, this approach is not authentic. Research has shown that students learn words more quickly when they are presented in context than when they are presented in isolation or in lists. The best way for students to learn to read many words is to encounter them repeatedly in the process of reading "connected text"—in other words, by reading real stories, poems, and books (Biemiller, 1977–1978; Perfetti, Finger, & Hogaboam, 1978; Stanovich, 1980).

There are many different lists of sight words that can be used for instruction. The most popular are the Dolch Sight Word List, the Fry Instant Word List, and the Bookwords list. Each of the lists is comprised of frequently used words; however, the lists are not identical. In general, sight words selected for instruction should be those that cannot be sounded out using phonics, are frequently found in reading material, and have a "high utility"—words that the students would want to write as well as read. Not all of the words on sight words lists meet each of these criteria, so teachers should pick and choose the words from the lists that do meet the criteria, and teach the others in more appropriate ways.

The Dolch Sight Word List was developed by Edward Dolch in about 1936. It was originally published in 1948. The list includes words that were most commonly used in children's reading materials of that time, so it is not always in synch with more current reading material. Despite its age, the Dolch list remains one of the most commonly used lists of sight words. It is conveniently divided into grade levels, providing guidance to teachers regarding the words that students of each level should know.

Teachers should keep in mind that the grade levels were determined at the time of the publication of the sight word lists, so they are also outdated and may not directly correspond with contemporary expectations of student achievement. The Dolch list does include some words that can be easily identified using phonics; these words should *not* be taught as sight words.

The Fry Instant Word List was devised by Edward B. Fry, and it was first published in an article in the journal *The Reading Teacher* in 1980. Fry's lists are convenient, as they are arranged in groups of 100 words. The words in the first list of 100 comprise 50 percent of all the words in written English. This makes these very important words for children to know on sight. The words in the first three lists (300 words) comprise 65 percent of all the words found in written English. As with the Dolch word lists, some of the words in the Fry lists are best introduced using phonics; teachers should teach these words using other word attack strategies and teach as sight words only those words that cannot be identified in any other way.

The Bookwords list was developed by Maryann Eeds and first published in *The Reading Teacher* in 1985. This list includes 227 high-frequency words that were the most common words found in books written for children. Whereas other lists of sight words commonly used basal reading series as a basis for identifying "high-frequency words," the Bookwords list used 400 of the most popular children's literature books as a basis for identifying the words on the list. This makes the Bookwords list very valuable for teachers who are teaching in a literature-based curriculum.

Links to each of these lists can be found in the Resources section of this chapter.

Grade Levels:	PK - 4
Materials Needed:	Copy of the target word list for each student
	Writing implement
Data Generated:	This assessment will generate lists of high-frequency words that the student can and cannot identify either in context or in isolation, depending upon the assessment approach used.
Data Usage:	Periodic assessment can be used to chart progress in students' knowledge of high-frequency sight words. In addition, assessment can identify unknown words that can be taught through meaningful, authentic literacy experiences.
Directions:	Teachers should keep a sight word list for each student. As the teacher works with each student during reading instruction, the teacher should select several words from the list that are present in the current story that is being read by the students. As each student reads, the teacher notes on the word list whether or not the word was correctly identified by each student. This approach is authentic and documents the students' ability to identify high-frequency sight words in context, which is what needs to be done in authentic reading situations.
	Conversely, teachers may also put the words on index cards or in short lists and ask the students to read the words in isolation. This is a nonauthentic assessment, and the results will not accurately mirror the students' ability to identify the words in context; however, it is a quick way to get an idea of the students' ability to identify many words in a short amount of time.
	Regardless of the manner in which the words are identified, instruction in sight word identification should occur through authentic experiences using meaningful text, not word lists or flash cards.

Assessment 7.2

Greene's Informal Word Analysis Inventory

Background:	Sylvia Greene's Informal Word Analysis Inventory is an informal assessment that is in the public domain.
Grade Levels:	All
Materials Needed:	Copies of the Learner and Teacher Word Lists at the appropriate level (I or II) for the student.
	Writing Implements
Data Generated:	This assessment will provide evidence regarding the student's ability to decode and encode words.
Data Usage:	Specific analysis of the data pinpoints sound/symbol correspondences that the student needs to learn or practice. Data can be used to build personalized spelling lists for students or to generate lists of patterns and sound/symbol correspondences that should be targeted in direct instruction lessons.
Directions:	Decoding: Students are given the appropriate list of words. As they read each word, the teacher notes the response. Incorrect responses are written down for additional analysis. For example, if the target word is "dog" and the student reads "down," the teacher should write down the word "down." These miscues can be analyzed for insight into the students' decoding strategies.
	Encoding: The teacher reads the words from the appropriate list, and the student writes them down, as if it was a typical spelling test. The student's spelling is then analyzed for information about his or her knowledge of sound/symbol correspondences.
Source:	http://lincs.ed.gov/readingprofiles/PF_SG_All_Docs.htm.

Greene's Informal Word Analysis Inventory

Student Copy Level I

DIRECTIONS: Read the words in each list from the top of the page to the bottom. If you aren't sure about a word, try to figure it out.

fan	thin	hung
hag	wham	brag
Sal	rum	slot
ban	cup	snap
tag	log	strut
rig	mod	sprig
Sid	fen	runt
shin	met	Fisk
chat	quit	Luke
pitch	quack	file
latch	rank	rote
sack	link	nape
bath	Kong	Pete

Greene's Informal Word Analysis Inventory
Student Copy Level II

DIRECTIONS: Read the words in each list from the top of the page to the bottom. If you aren't sure about a word, try to figure it out.

vain	**gauze**	**mild**
jay	**jaw**	**cent**
peek	**knack**	**pace**
beam	**writ**	**cinch**
roam	**tight**	**cyst**
mow	**limb**	**gem**
foe	**sly**	**binge**
hue	**tie**	**gin**
few	**hark**	**gym**
void	**port**	**phase**
soy	**verb**	**tough**
foul	**firm**	**deaf**
pow	**curl**	**hunted**
loop	**pall**	**wished**
hood	**balm**	**slammed**

Greene's Informal Word Analysis Inventory

Teacher's Copy Level I

DIRECTIONS: Put a check in the columns "reading" and "spelling" after the words on the list that are read or spelled correctly. For those that are incorrect, write down the student's attempt at reading or spelling that word.

Word	Reading	Spelling
fan		
hag		
Sal		
ban		
tag		
rig		
Sid		
shin		
chat		
pitch		
latch		
sack		
bath		

Word	Reading	Spelling
thin		
wham		
rum		
cup		
log		
mod		
fen		
met		
quit		
quack		
rank		
link		
Kong		

Word	Reading	Spelling
hung		
brag		
slot		
snap		
strut		
sprig		
runt		
Fisk		
Luke		
file		
rote		
nape		
Pete		

Greene's Informal Word Analysis Inventory

Teacher's Copy Level II

DIRECTIONS: Put a check in the columns "reading" and "spelling" after the words on the list that are read or spelled correctly. For those that are incorrect, write down the student's attempt at reading or spelling that word.

Word	Reading	Spelling	Sound/Symbol Correspondences
vain			vowel digraph ai, initial /v/, final /n/
jay			vowel digraph ay, initial /j/
peek			vowel digraph ee, initial /p/, final /k/
beam			vowel digraph ea, initial /b/, final /m/
roam			vowel digraph oa, initial /r/, final /m/
mow			diphthong ow as long o, initial /m/
foe			initial /f/, silent e with long o
hue			initial /h/, silent e with long u
few			initial /f/, diphthong ew
void			initial /v/, final /d/, diphthong oi
soy			initial /s/, diphthong oy
foul			initial /f/, final /l/, diphthong ou
pow			initial /p/, diphthong ow
loop			initial /l/, final /p/, double oo (long)
hood			initial /h/, final /d/, double oo (short)

Word	Reading	Spelling	Sound/Symbol Correspondences
gauze			initial /g/, final /z/, vowel digraph au, silent e
jaw			initial /j/, diphthong aw
knack			kn (silent k), short a, final ck
writ			wr (silent w), short i, final /t/
tight			initial /t/, -ight rime (silent gh)
limb			initial /l/, short i, mb (silent b)
sly			initial sl blend, final y as long i
tie			initial /t/, long i with silent e
hark			initial /h/, -ark rime, r-controlled a
port			initial /p/, r-controlled o, final /t/
verb			initial /v/, r-controlled e, final /b/
firm			initial /f/, r-controlled i, final /m/
curl			initial hard c /k/, r-controlled u, final /l/
pall			initial /p/, -all rime
balm			initial /b/, lm (silent l)

Word	Reading	Spelling	Sound/Symbol Correspondences
mild			initial /m/, ld (silent l)
cent			initial soft c /s/, -ent rime
pace			initial /p/, -ace rime, final soft c /s/
cinch			initial soft c /s/, -inch rime, ch digraph
cyst			initial soft c /s/, y as long i, final /st/ blend
gem			initial soft g /j/, -em rime, ge- (soft)
binge			initial /b/, short i, medial soft g /j/, silent e
gin			initial soft g /j/, -in rime, gi- (soft)
gym			initial soft g /j/, gy-(soft), y as long i, final /m/
phase			digraph ph /f/, long a with silent e
tough			initial /t/, -ough rime, digraph gh /f/
deaf			initial /d/, vowel digraph ea (short), final /f/
hunted			-ed as "ed," initial /h/, -unt rime
wished			-ed as "t," initial /w/, -ish rime
slammed			-ed as "d," initial sl blend, -am rime, double medial consonants before adding ending

Greene's Informal Word Analysis Inventory
Student Copy Level II

DIRECTIONS: Read the words in each list from the top of the page to the bottom. If you aren't sure about a word, try to figure it out.

vain	**gauze**	**mild**
jay	**jaw**	**cent**
peek	**knack**	**pace**
beam	**writ**	**cinch**
roam	**tight**	**cyst**
mow	**limb**	**gem**
foe	**sly**	**binge**
hue	**tie**	**gin**
few	**hark**	**gym**
void	**port**	**phase**
soy	**verb**	**tough**
foul	**firm**	**deaf**
pow	**curl**	**hunted**
loop	**pall**	**wished**
hood	**balm**	**slammed**

Additional Word Skills and Strategies Assessments

CORE Phonics Survey
http://www.senia.asia/wp-content/uploads/2011/02/CORE-Phonics-Survey-Scholastic.pdf.

Word Reading Test
http://lincs.ed.gov/readingprofiles/FT_WRT_intro.htm.

Phonics Assessment (nonsense words) "BAF Test"
http://www.saveteacherssundays.com/uploads/Phonics%20assessment%20(using%20non-words).pdf.

Primary Phonics Assessment
http://phonemicsinadigitalage.weebly.com/uploads/1/1/3/6/1136348/guidelinesforassesseingphonics
.pdf.

Word Skills and Strategies Resources

Dolch Word List
http://bogglesworldesl.com/dolch/lists.htm.

The Fry Instant Word List
http://bjh.dadeschools.net/assets/fry_complete_1000.pdf.

Bookwords List
http://www.jstor.org/discover/10.2307/20198802?uid=3739864&uid=2129&uid=2&uid=70&uid
=4&uid=3739256&sid=21102160819293.

Tips for Teaching Word Recognition
https://www.readinga-z.com/tutoring-mentoring-packs/tips-phonics.pdf.

37 Most Useful Rimes (Make over 500 words)
http://cbl.jordandistrict.org/files/37commonrimes1.pdf.

Word Skills and Strategies Assessment and Instruction Matrix

Skill/Concept	Assessment	Development Activities
Identifying Sight Words	7.1	Language Experience Approach
		Word Walls
		Morning Message
		Big Books with Pointers/Shared Reading
		Sight Word Bingo
		Sight Word Concentration
		Sight Word Scavenger Hunt
Word Analysis	7.2	Letter/Sound Collages
		Beginning/Ending Sound Bingo
		Onset/Rime Slides
		Onset/Rime Flip Books
		Onset/Rimes in Nursery Rhymes and Poems
		Word Building with Letter Cubes
		Word Sorting
		Making Words
		Making and Writing Words
		Spelling-Based Word Sorts
		Making Words Grow
		Analogic Phonics
		Collecting Words
		Logographic Word Cards

Chapter Activities

1. Administer a sight word assessment for a student (Gr. K-4), following the directions for Assessment 7.1.
    a. Explain why you chose the sight words you used for the assessment.
    b. Write a one- to two-page summary of the results of the assessment.
    c. Describe an activity that you would implement to support the assessed student's sight word development. Be specific regarding the words you would use for the activity and what the student would do during the activity. Write a paragraph explaining the rationale for your selection of the words and the activity.
2. Administer the Greene's Informal Word Analysis Inventory. Analyze the student's responses. Identify patterns that the student knows and needs to learn. Select three patterns the student needs to practice, and suggest one instructional activity you would use for that pattern. Also identify a text that could be used with the student to practice that pattern in meaningful context.

References

Biemiller, A. (1977–1978). Relationship between oral reading rates for letters, words, and simple text in the development of reading achievement. *Reading Research Quarterly, 13,* 223–253.

Perfetti, C. A., Finger, E. & Hogaboam, T. W. (1978). Sources of vocalization latency differences between skilled and less skilled young readers. *Journal of Educational Psychology, 70,* 730–739.

Stanovich, K. E. (1980). Toward an interactive-compensatory model of individual differences in the development of reading fluency. *Reading Research Quarterly, 16,* 32–71.

© photographer/Shutterstock.com

Informal Literacy Assessments: Spelling

Spelling

Spelling and phonics are reciprocal processes. Spelling involves thinking of a sound and then deciding on how to represent that sound with written symbols. Phonics involves looking at written symbols and then deciding what sound(s) to give them. Because of the close relationship between spelling and phonics, assessing students' spelling not only gives us information about spelling development but also provides invaluable information that can be used to teach students about word identification in reading.

This chapter will focus on assessing spelling developmentally, according to stages identified by research. In addition, instructional approaches for enhancing spelling and word identification development, such as *Words Their Way*, will be described.

Assessments included in this chapter are as follows:

Assessment 8.1   Developmental Spelling Assessment

Assessment 8.2   Assessing Spelling Using Writing Samples

Developmental Spelling Assessment

Background

Spelling instruction has traditionally been one of the most overlooked areas in language arts. In many classrooms, spelling "instruction" consists of assigning a list of words to be learned for the week, followed by a spelling test on Friday. This approach to teaching spelling generally does not support spelling development; most of the words that adults can spell correctly were not those they learned on spelling tests in elementary school!

If teachers want students to become proficient spellers, they must implement spelling instruction that provides students with the tools they need to learn about spelling as they read and write. Effective spelling instruction focuses on the development of students' knowledge of orthographic (spelling) patterns. Students must learn common orthographic patterns in English and learn to look for them in words as they are reading. In turn, this will support their use of these patterns when they write. Researchers have identified five stages of spelling development through which students progress on their way to becoming proficient spellers. These stages are: pre-phonemic, phonemic/letter-name, within-word pattern, syllables and affixes, and derivational relations.

Grade Levels:	PK–12
Materials Needed:	Developmental Spelling Assessment
	Developmental Spelling Assessment Scoring Guide
	Writing implement
Data Generated:	Assessment will identify the student's developmental spelling stage.
Data Usage:	Once the teacher has identified each student's developmental spelling stage, this information can be used to appropriately match the student with instruction that will support his or her development and help move to the next stage.
Directions:	Read each word on the spelling list. Ask students to spell each word. Use the Developmental Spelling Assessment Scoring Guide to assess the student's spelling and to identify his or her developmental spelling level.

Developmental Spelling Assessment

Read the word, then the sentence that uses the word. Ask the student to write the word.

Primary List (Grades K–2)

1. **gate**   I opened the **gate** so I could walk up the sidewalk.
2. **pink**   **Pink** is my mother's favorite color.
3. **ship**   The space**ship** flew to the moon.
4. **please**   **Please** be sure to put your name on your paper.
5. **jumped**   The dog **jumped** over the little stream.
6. **bell**   The **bell** rang to signal the end of recess.
7. **shirts**   I have three blue **shirts** to wear to school.
8. **once**   I **once** visited the state of Florida.
9. **heard**   The boy **heard** the bees buzzing on the flowers.
10. **stamped**   She **stamped** the letter before mailing it.
11. **trade**   Will you **trade** your cupcake for my cookies?
12. **third**   The baseball player made it to **third** base.
13. **chick**   A baby chicken is called a **chick**.
14. **rain**   The soccer game was cancelled because of the **rain**.
15. **shrimp**   A **shrimp** is a small sea creature.
16. **looked**   I **looked** both ways before crossing the street.

Intermediate List (Grades 3–up)

1. letter   I will mail the **letter** at the post office.
2. glove   In a baseball game, the catcher wears a **glove**.
3. flowery   My grandmother wore a **flowery** dress.
4. sign   **Sign** your name on the line.
5. mutton   **Mutton** is a type of meat that comes from sheep.
6. sailor   A **sailor** in the Navy works on a ship.
7. mission   The spy went on a top-secret **mission**.
8. feature   The **feature** story in a newspaper is on page one.
9. reeked   He smelled bad because he **reeked** of onions.
10. special   Meatloaf was today's lunch **special.**
11. teacher   My **teacher** never assigns homework on Friday.
12. glowed   The candle in the pumpkin **glowed** eerily.
13. pail   I used a shovel and **pail** to build a sand castle.
14. creature   Frankenstein is a scary **creature!**
15. hatter   The Mad **Hatter** met Alice in Wonderland.
16. signature   Your **signature** should be in cursive.
17. illustrate Please draw a picture to **illustrate** your story.

Developmental Spelling Assessment
Scoring Guide

Student _____ Grade _____ Date _____

Primary List (Grades K–2)
Spelling Levels

Prompt	Student Spelling	1	2	3	4	5	6
gate							
pink							
ship							
please							
jumped							
bell							
shirts							
once							
heard							
stamped							
trade							
third							
chick							
rain							
shrimp							
looked							
alone							
split							
phone							
into							

Developmental Levels   # of responses

1. Pre-phonemic   _____ × 1 = _____
2. Phonemic/Letter Name   _____ × 2 = _____
3. Within Word   _____ × 3 = _____
4. Syllables and Affixes   _____ × 4 = _____
5. Derivational Relations _____ × 5 = _____
6. Conventional (correct) _____ × 6 = _____

Total: _____/20 = *_____

* This number will be a number between 1 and 6, for example, 2.3 or 3.7.
This indicates the average of the responses and provides an estimate of the student's current developmental spelling level.

Student's Developmental Spelling Level: _____

Developmental Spelling Assessment

Scoring Guide

Student _____ Grade _____ Date _____

Intermediate List (Grades 3–up)

Prompt	Student Spelling	1	2	3	4	5	6
letter							
glove							
flowery							
sign							
mutton							
sailor							
mission							
feature							
reeked							
special							
teacher							
glowed							
pail							
creature							
hatter							
signature							
illustrate							
knife							
wraith							
middle							

Developmental Levels	# of responses	
1. Pre-phonemic	_____ x 1 =	_____
2. Phonemic/Letter Name	_____ x 2 =	_____
3. Within Word	_____ x 3 =	_____
4. Syllables and Affixes	_____ x 4 =	_____
5. Derivational Relations	_____ x 5 =	_____
6. Conventional (correct)	_____ x 6 =	_____
	Total: _____/20 = *_____	

* This number will be a number between 1 and 6, for example, 2.3 or 3.7.
This indicates the average of the responses and provides an estimate of the student's current developmental spelling level.

Student's Developmental Spelling Level: _____

Developmental Spelling Stages

Pre-Phonemic Stage

- Students are not aware of the alphabetic principle.
- Letter-like forms may be used in place of real letters.
- Combinations of letters and numbers may be seen.
- Individual letters are used to represent syllables or whole words.
- Initial sounds are not always represented.
- Final sounds are not always represented.
- Vowel elements are not represented.

Phonemic /Letter Name Stage/Alphabetic

- Students are aware of the alphabetic principle.
- At early stages, may use single letters to represent whole words
- At later stages, represents initial and final consonant sounds
- At early stages, short vowels are represented by the letter name for the long vowel that is formed in approximately the same place in the mouth as the short vowel that the student is trying to spell—typically:

  short *e* is spelled with an *a*
  short *i* is spelled with an *e*
  short *o* is spelled with an *i*
  short *u* is spelled with an *o*

- Toward the end of the stage, short vowels are spelled correctly.
- Long vowels are represented by letter names.
- *-ed* endings are spelled by sound (e.g., "helped" would be "helpt").
- Beginning and ending consonant sounds are generally consistent.
- All phonemes are usually represented, although some may be unconventional,
- Uses the letter *r* to represent *r*-controlled vowels.
- Sounds of /ch/ and /j/ are not correctly represented.
- Pre-consonant nasal sounds are not represented (m, n) especially when they appear before a consonant (e.g., "cap" instead of "camp").

Within-Word Pattern Stage

- V-C-e pattern is used.
- Irregular but highly frequent patterns (e.g., –*ight*) are spelled correctly.
- Inflectional endings are correct.
- Short vowel sounds are correct.
- Consonant clusters begin to appear correctly (e.g., spr-).
- Vowels are present in every syllable.
- R-controlled vowel patterns are represented, but not always correctly.

- Long vowels are represented, but not always correctly.
- Complex consonant units are not accurately represented (e.g., –*tch*).
- Schwa sounds in unaccented syllables are not accurately represented.
- Begin to use visual features (orthographic knowledge) as well as sound features in order to spell words—spelling is no longer based only on sound.
- Begin to show use of rules, such as final e and double vowel letters (vowel digraphs), to spell long vowel sounds.
- A sign that a student is in the stage is the inclusion of silent letters in spelling.
- Most one-syllable words are spelled correctly.
- Students with poor orthographic knowledge begin to have difficulty with spelling at this level.

Syllables and Affixes Stage

- Single syllables in words are spelled correctly.
- Long vowel patterns are applied to multisyllabic words.
- R-controlled patterns are applied to multisyllabic words.
- Evidence of doubling rules when adding suffixes.
- Evidence of "dropping e" rules when adding suffixes, such as dropping the final e when adding –ing, such as in "dating."
- Vowel patterns in unstressed syllables are not accurately represented (e.g., soler for solar).

Derivational Relations Stage

- Mastery of two and three syllable words.
- Prefixes characterized by double consonants (e.g., illiterate and irrelevant) are correctly represented.
- Root words represented in terms of meaning.
- Students apply the "principle of meaning"—words that have similar meanings are spelled similarly, even though pronunciations may be different (e.g., sign, signal).

Conventional Stage

- Most words are spelled correctly, according to the conventions of the society.

Based on: Gunning, 2006, Young, 2007

Assessing Spelling Using Writing Samples

Background

Assessing students' spelling developmentally does not require that the teacher spend valuable instructional time administering a special spelling assessment. It is possible to utilize students' writing samples from class assignments, writing portfolios, journals, and so on to analyze students' spelling. When this approach is used, it is necessary to make sure that you have a sufficient number of words or the results may be skewed. For example, a teacher who assesses the spelling of a first-grade student, using only one writing sample of five or six words, will find that the assessment will not be accurate. It is suggested that in order to obtain an adequate analysis, the writing samples used should contain at least 40–50 words for students in grades K–2 and at least 80–100 words for students in third grade or higher.

In addition to identifying the overall developmental spelling level, this analysis can also provide information regarding patterns in students' spelling errors.

This approach can be inaccurate when working with students who insist on writing only words that they can spell. Teachers should watch for this issue when analyzing students' spelling.

Grade Levels:	PK–12
Materials Needed:	Student Writing Samples
	Developmental Spelling Analysis Form
	Writing implement
Data Generated:	Assessment will identify the student's developmental spelling stage.
Data Usage:	Once the teacher has identified each student's developmental spelling stage, this information can be used to appropriately match the student with instruction that will support his or her development and support movement to the next stage.
Directions:	Use a collection of students' writing samples from a journal or writing portfolio to identify students' developmental spelling levels. Complete the Developmental Spelling Analysis Form for each student.

Developmental Spelling Analysis Form for Student Writing Samples

Student _____ Grade _____ Date _____

Spelling Level

Actual Word	Student Spelling	1	2	3	4	5	6

Developmental Levels	# of responses	
1. Pre-phonemic	_____ × 1 =	_____
2. Phonemic/Letter Name	_____ × 2 =	_____
3. Within Word	_____ × 3 =	_____
4. Syllables and Affixes	_____ × 4 =	_____
5. Derivational Relations	_____ × 5 =	_____
6. Conventional (correct)	_____ × 6 =	_____

Total: _____/N = *_____

N = total number of words in writing sample. Use more than one sheet, if needed, and do not calculate the developmental level until all the words have been tallied.

* This number will be a number between 1 and 6, for example, 2.3 or 3.7. This indicates the average of the responses and provides an estimate of the student's current developmental spelling level.

Student's Developmental Spelling Level: _____

Monitoring Spelling Development over Time

Rather than assessing students' spelling on the basis of a weekly spelling test, it is more useful for instructional purposes to assess students' writing using writing samples or developmental spelling assessments once each month. Growth can then be charted to demonstrate that the students' spelling is progressing through the developmental stages.

If a weekly spelling test is expected (by parents or administrators), teachers should select words for each student that focus on the patterns and spelling knowledge needed to move the student from his or her current developmental stage to the following stage. Because this process can be time-consuming, there are some developmentally based spelling programs, such as *Words Their Way,* which provide teachers with developmental assessments and lists of words for spelling instruction.

Words Their Way

Words Their Way is a research-based, developmental spelling program developed by Bear, Invernizzi, Templeton, and Johnston. It is used widely in elementary schools as a spelling curriculum. The program provides progressively more difficult word lists for teachers to use as students progress through the stages of spelling development. The program is individualized; students work on word lists that match their current developmental spelling level. Program activities stress word-sorting activities that direct students' attention to the similarities and differences among words.

Numerous resources are available online to support the use of Words Their Way in the classroom, ranging from professionally published commercial materials to teacher-made materials freely shared on websites. Spelling lists, word sorts, board games, and electronic games are all available. Some useful websites have been included in the Spelling Resources section of this chapter.

Additional Spelling Assessments

Gentry and Gillet Developmental Spelling Test ("Monster" Test)
https://www.hasdk12.org/cms/lib/PA01001366/Centricity/Domain/5/Monster%20Spelling%20Test
.pdf.

Primary and Elementary Spelling Inventories
http://www.warrencountyschools.org/userfiles/2185/Classes/160244/wtw%20spelling%20inventory
.pdf?id=600944.

McGuffey Qualitative Spelling Inventory (useful for older students)
http://gn009.k12.sd.us/ELL%20Resources/Words%20Their%20Way%20Resources/Assessments/
McGuffey%20Qualitative%20Spelling%20Inventory.pdf.

Spelling Resources

Words Their Way Overview
https://www.pearsonschool.com/index.cfm?locator=PS2sIb&elementType=news&elemen
tId=267212.

Words Their Way Parent Informational Brochure
http://www.coppellisd.com/cms/lib07/TX01000550/Centricity/domain/975/shared/wordstheirway
.pdf.

Spelling Assessment and Instruction Matrix

Developmental Level	Assessment	Instructional Focus and Activities
Pre-phonemic	8.1, 8.2	Big Books/Shared Reading
		Language Experience Approach
		Letter/Sound Matching
		Letter/Sound Concentration
		Writing Using Invented Spelling
		Letter/Sound Collages
		Songs/Poems
Phonemic/Letter Name		CVC Flip Books
		Word Building Tiles/Cards
		Onset/Rimes Flip Books (CVC)
		Onset/Rimes Slides (CVC)
		Onset/Rimes Wheels (CVC)
		Writing Using Invented Spelling
		Word Sorts
Within Word		Onset/Rimes Flip Books (CVVC)
		Onset/Rimes Wheels (CVVC)
		Onset/Rimes Slides (CVCC)
		Writing Using Invented Spelling
		Word Sorts
		Homophone Activities
Syllables and Affixes		Adding Inflectional Endings
		Common Prefixes/Suffixes
		Homographs and Accent/Stress
		Consonant Doubling
		Making Words Grow
		Word Sorts/Board Games
Derivational Relations		Silent Letters
		Vowel Alternation Patterns
		Consonant Alternation Patterns
		Word Detectives
		Word Sorts/Board Games

Chapter Activities

1. Review the Gentry and Gillet "Monster Test," at the link that is listed in the Additional Spelling Assessments section of this chapter. Notice that Gentry and Gillet provide sample spellings for each word to correspond with each of the spelling developmental stages. Select one of the word lists used in Assessment 8.1. Develop a chart indicating at least one possible spelling for each word for each of the developmental levels.
2. Compare a traditional spelling curriculum lesson and weekly word list with a Words Their Way list and lesson. What benefits/drawbacks do you see to each approach?
3. Use the following two writing samples to assess Mark's developmental spelling level. Use the Developmental Spelling Analysis Form from Assessment 8.2 to calculate his developmental level.

Writing Sample 1

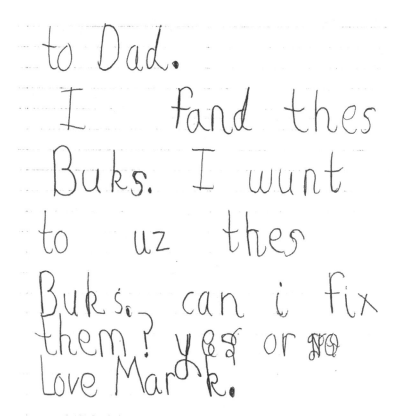

Contributed by Mark Robbins © Kendall Hunt Publishing Company

Writing Sample 2

Contributed by Mark Robbins © Kendall Hunt Publishing Company

References

Bear, D., et al. (2011). *Words Their Way: Study for Phonics, Vocabulary and Spelling Instruction, 4E.* Boston: Pearson.

Gunning, T. G. (2006). *Assessing and Correcting Reading and Writing Difficulties.* Boston: Allyn & Bacon, 142–244.

Young, K. (2007). Developmental Stage Theory of Spelling: Analysis of Consistency Across Four Spelling-Related Activities. *Australian Journal of Language and Literacy,* 30(3), 203–220.

© photographer/Shutterstock.com

Informal Literacy Assessments: Fluency

Fluency Is More Than Speed

Many teachers assess students' reading fluency by utilizing timed assessments, which stress the student's reading speed and accuracy in word identification. These assessments do not assess all the important facets of fluency. Fluency is more than reading fast; in fact, sometimes it is necessary to consciously read slowly in order to read a text fluently!

Fluency is the ability to read expressively, meaningfully, accurately, and with *appropriate* speed. When fluency assessments focus solely on how fast children can read, children begin to believe that reading fast is what is important. This belief can actually inhibit effective fluency development.

The assessments discussed in this chapter will allow teachers to view fluency in a multidimensional manner, considering all the important facets of fluency, not just speed.

Elements of Fluency

Some of the elements of fluency that should be assessed and taught in fluency activities in the classroom are as follows:

- Smoothness
- Phrasing
- Rate
- Accuracy
- Expression

Multidimensional Fluency Assessment

Background:	Using a rubric to assess fluency assures that the assessor is focusing on each of the important facets that contribute to fluency: reading rate, accuracy, expression, smoothness, and phrasing.
Grade Levels:	1–12
Materials Needed:	Multi-Dimensional Fluency Assessment Rubric Writing implement
Data Generated:	The multidimensional rubric will yield one holistic fluency score that considers each of the dimensions that contribute to fluent reading.
Data Usage:	Data can be used to track students' fluency development and to identify the dimensions of fluency that should be targeted for instruction.
Directions:	1. Provide the student with a passage to read orally. The passage should be on the student's independent reading level or should be a text that has been previously read in an instructional setting.
	2. Listen to the student read the passage orally, and assess the student's reading fluency using the multidimensional rubric. Make comments to remind yourself of specific strengths or needs so that you can develop formative feedback to give the student about his or her reading. *Note*: The student's reading can also be recorded so that the teacher and student can listen to it together prior to the teacher's giving the formative feedback. The *Rating* is the average of the individual dimension scores.
	3. Assess the student's reading once each week or at least every other week throughout the academic year to note his or her progress and to monitor fluency development over time.

Multi-Dimensional Fluency Rubric

Student _____ Grade _____

	Rate (R)	Accuracy (A)	Expression (E)	Smoothness (S)	Phrasing (P)
1.	slow/laborious	struggles with identification of many words	very little expression; monotone	long pauses; very choppy	word-by-word; no phrasing
2.	slower than appropriate	sounds out many words	mostly monotone; uses only basic punctuation	some pauses; somewhat choppy	some word-by-word; some 2–3 word phrases
3.	rate varies between slow and appropriate	sounds out a few words; limited disruption; self-corrects	some monotone; some use of appropriate expression; greater use of punctuation	few pauses; may be choppy in one or two places	mostly phrases
4.	rate mostly appropriate; sounds conversational	knows most words on sight; may still have to decode some more difficult words; may have some self-corrections	generally uses punctuation appropriately; good expression	almost no pauses; reading sounds smooth	appropriate phrasing in almost all cases
5.	maintains appropriate rate throughout; sounds conversational	limited use of word analysis; few self-corrections	consistent and appropriate use of punctuation; meaningful expression	reading sounds very smooth	consistent use of appropriate phrasing

Date   Text   Text   Individual Element Scores

                                                          Level   R   A   E   S   P

___   _____   ____   ____   ____   ____   ____   ____

___   _____   ____   ____   ____   ____   ____   ____

___   _____   ____   ____   ____   ____   ____   ____

___   _____   ____   ____   ____   ____   ____   ____

___   _____   ____   ____   ____   ____   ____   ____

___   _____   ____   ____   ____   ____   ____   ____

___   _____   ____   ____   ____   ____   ____   ____

___   _____   ____   ____   ____   ____   ____   ____

___   _____   ____   ____   ____   ____   ____   ____

Fluency Self-Assessment and Peer Assessment

Background: Reading fluency continues to develop as students gain experience reading a variety of texts. Students need to learn to listen to their own oral reading so that they can monitor and adjust their rate and evaluate their phrasing and use of expression. Having students self-assess their own reading fluency and assess the reading fluency of a reading partner can help them learn to "hear" what fluent reading sounds like, so that they know when they are reading fluently themselves.

Grade Levels: 1–12

Materials Needed: How Well Did Your Partner Read? handout

Writing Implement

Data Generated: This assessment will provide the teacher with information about a student's ability to assess his or her own fluent reading and to recognize the aspects of fluent reading in the oral reading of others.

Data Usage: Data can be used to track students' fluency development and to identify the dimensions of fluency that should be targeted for instruction.

Directions:
1. Students should complete the How Well Did Your Partner Read? activity at the end of each week as they are working with partners during partner-reading activities.

2. Teachers should compare the students' self- and peer-assessments with their own fluency assessments for each student in order to judge students' ability to recognize the elements of fluent reading in their own oral reading and in the reading of others.

3. Data gathered from this assessment can be used to plan students' fluency activities so that their self-established goals are supported by instruction.

How Well Did You and Your Partner Read?

(Adapted from Johns & Berglund (2002). *Fluency: Questions, Answers, Evidence-Based Strategies.* Dubuque, IA: Kendall-Hunt Publishing.)

Name: _____

Partner's Name: _____

Date: _____

We read _____

My Partner's Reading

Put an X on the lines that describe what your partner did while reading:

_____ Read smoothly   _____ Did not read too slowly or too fast

_____ Knew most of the words   _____ Sounded like he or she was talking

_____ Used punctuation clues   _____ Read phrases, not word-by-word

Put a star next to *one* of the reading behaviors above that *your partner* did better than the last time you read together.

My Reading

Put an X on the lines that describe what *you* did while reading today:

_____ Read smoothly   _____ Did not read too slowly or too fast

_____ Knew most of the words   _____ Sounded like he or she was talking

_____ Used punctuation clues   _____ Read phrases, not word-by-word

Put a star next to *one* of the reading behaviors above that *you* did better than the last time you read together.

Planning for Next Time

Put an X on the line to show one thing that you and your partner will work on improving the next time you read together:

_____ Knowing the words   _____ Using good expression

_____ Reading words in phrases   _____ Using punctuation correctly

_____ Sounding like talking   _____ Reading at the right speed

_____ Reading more smoothly   _____ Sounding like the character

Fluency Assessment Rubric

(Adapted from Johns & Berglund (2002). *Fluency: Questions, Answers, Evidence-Based Strategies.* Dubuque, IA: Kendall-Hunt Publishing.)

Student _____ Grade _____

Fluency Scale

1. Word-by-word, long pauses between words, struggles with many words, reads in a monotone voice, little evidence of use of punctuation, rate is generally slow

2. Some word-by-word reading, some two- to three-word phrases, some hesitations, sounds out many words, which disrupts flow, reads mostly in monotone, shows some basic use of punctuation, slower rate than appropriate

3. Mostly reads in phrases, some word-by-word, some smooth, some choppy, combines appropriate use of expression with some monotone, shows some use of punctuation but still ignores some, rate varies between slow and acceptable

4. Mostly reads in phrases, generally smooth, may exhibit difficulty with some difficult words, uses appropriate expression throughout most of the passage, uses punctuation appropriately, rate is generally conversational

5. Appropriate phrasing is consistently used, generally smooth, limited use of self-corrections, appropriate expression and intonation maintained throughout, uses punctuation consistently, rate is conversational and consistent

Date	Rating	Level	Text
____	____	____	_____
____	____	____	_____
____	____	____	_____
____	____	____	_____
____	____	____	_____
____	____	____	_____

Additional Fluency Assessments

NAEP Oral Reading Fluency Scale

https://nces.ed.gov/nationsreportcard/studies/ors/scale.aspx.

Rubric for Oral Reading Fluency

https://dese.mo.gov/sites/default/files/ela-6-my_portfolio_anecdotal-summative_assessment_2-oral_reading_fluency_rubric.pdf.

Fluency Resources

Books

Johns, J. & Berglund, R.L. (2010). Fluency: Differentiated Interventions and Progress-Monitoring Assessments. Dubuque, IA: Kendall Hunt. ISBN-13: 978-0757593611.

Rasinski, T.V. & Smith, M.C. (2018). *The Megabook of Fluency*. New York: Scholastic. ISBN-13: 978-1338257014.

Websites

Reader's Theater: A Reason to Read Aloud

http://www.educationworld.com/a_curr/profdev/profdev082.shtml.

Five Surefire Strategies for Developing Reading Fluency

http://www.scholastic.com/teachers/article/5-surefire-strategies-developing-reading-fluency.

Videos

Fluency and Word Study (Grades 3–5)

http://www.learner.org/workshops/teachreading35/session2/.

Fluency Assessment and Instruction Matrix

Fluency Element	Assessment	Development Activities
Appropriate Rate	9.1 and 9.2	Repeated Reading for Performance
		Choral Reading
		Readers' Theater
		Partner Reading
		Antiphonal Reading
		Radio Reading
		Word Theater
		Recorded Books
Expression	9.1 and 9.2	Choral Reading
		Readers' Theater
		Partner Reading
		Radio Reading
		Echo Reading
		Say It Like the Character
Phrasing	9.1 & 9.2	Supra-segmental Phonemes
		Choral Reading
		Antiphonal Reading
		Echo Reading
		Clustering Activities
		Phrase-Cued Text
		Fluency Fast Phrases

Note: Almost every fluency-focused instructional activity addresses a variety of elements; activities are listed with those elements most directly impacted by them.

Chapter Activities

1. Practice using the Multi-Dimensional Fluency Rubric to assess a student's reading.
   a. Identify the rating the student would receive for each of the fluency elements.
   b. Write down at least two pieces of formative feedback that you would give to the student based on the oral reading assessment. Be sure these are *specific* to the actual reading you assessed, not general statements.
2. After you have assessed a student using the Multi-Dimensional Fluency Rubric, identify at least two instructional strategies that would support the student's development of the elements of oral reading fluency. Explain your rationale for selecting those assessments.

References

Johns, J. & Berglund, R.L. (2002). *Fluency: Questions, Answers, Evidence-Based Strategies*. Dubuque, IA: Kendall-Hunt Publishing.

U.S. Dept. of Education, Institute of Education Sciences, National Center for Education Statistics, National Assessment of Educational Progress (NAEP), *2002 Oral Reading Study*. Retrieved from: http://nces.ed.gov/nationsreportcard/studies/ors/scale.aspx.

© photographer/Shutterstock.com

Informal Literacy Assessments: Comprehension and Strategy Usage

Comprehension

Since comprehension is the ultimate goal of all reading, assessing students' reading comprehension should be of primary importance to all teachers. Reading comprehension assessments that focus on what students *remember* from a text are typical; however, these are insufficient to assess all aspects of comprehension. Since one of the purposes of assessment is to inform instruction, it is also important to determine what *strategies* and *processes* the students use to form their understandings of a text. These aspects of comprehension are more difficult to assess; however, unless the teacher obtains this information about students, he or she will be unable to adequately teach them to become better readers.

This chapter includes assessments to assess students':

- Knowledge/memory of story elements
- Knowledge/memory of story structure
- Knowledge/memory of text structure in informational text
- Use of informational text features
- Ability to summarize informational text
- Use of comprehension strategies
- Ability to answer questions about text

Assessment 10.1

Using Retellings to Assess Knowledge of Story Elements and Plot

Background

Asking students to retell a story that they have read is an effective way to gauge their understanding and memory of the story elements and the basic plot. Retellings for this purpose are based on narrative text (stories). There are two types of rubrics that can be used to assess a student's retelling—generic retelling rubrics and story-specific retelling rubrics.

Generic retelling rubrics are rubrics that can be used with any story. The criteria identified in the cells of the rubric are general and nonspecific. These rubrics require less preassessment preparation by the teacher, as the same rubric can be used over and over with virtually all narrative text; however, they can be more difficult to use for the actual assessment, because of the vagueness of the listed criteria. For example, one cell in a generic retelling rubric might say, "Named all major characters," it does not name the characters. The teacher needs to remember the main characters in the story and make sure the student named all of them.

A story-specific retelling rubric makes the actual assessment process much easier for the teacher. Although these rubrics must be prepared by the teacher in advance of the retelling assessment, they can be used again with other students who read the same story. The specificity of the criteria named in the story-specific retelling rubric makes it more likely that the assessment will be both valid and reliable.

Grade Levels:	K–12
Materials Needed:	Retelling Rubric Materials
	Writing Implement
Data Generated:	A retelling rubric will provide data related to the student's memory of the story elements and the plot of the story.
Data Usage:	Data can be used to identify the student's ability to retell a story plot in sequence. In addition, data will indicate the student's awareness of and memory for story elements (plot, characters, etc.). Students who are unable to retell the plot in sequence or who do not remember important story elements can receive instruction focusing on those aspects of comprehension.

Directions:

Generic Retelling Rubric

1. After the student finishes reading the story *silently*, ask the student to retell the story, including as much of the story as he or she can remember.

2. Write down or record the student's retelling so that you can adequately assess it. When you are experienced at assessing retellings and are familiar with the rubric, you may be able to assess the student's retelling by recording it verbatim. You may also use the retelling record sheet for the appropriate type of text.

3. Use the generic retelling rubric to assign a score for each of the assessed areas. Add the student's score in each area to get the overall score to record on the chart.

Story-Specific Retelling Rubric

1. Use the story-specific retelling rubric outline to develop a story-specific rubric for the text that the student will be retelling.

2. Assign points to each of the items listed in the rubric. You may want to include additional points for having each plot event in sequence.

3. After the student finishes reading the story *silently*, ask him or her to retell the story. Check off each item on the rubric as it is mentioned by the student.

4. Complete the Story-Specific Retelling Summary Sheet for each student every time you assess a retelling. This sheet will allow you to see at a glance which of the story elements the student is having difficulty remembering and will allow you to tailor instruction to work on that element.

Generic Retelling Rubric

Student _____ Grade _____

Story Element	Level 1 Basic	Level 2 Average	Level 3 Advanced
Characters (C)	Student names the main character(s) only.	Student names main character(s) and some supporting characters.	Student names main characters and all supporting characters.
Setting (S)	Student makes a general reference to the setting.	Student refers specifically to the setting, naming time or place but not both.	Student specifically names both the time and place of the story.
Plot (P)	Student names at least three events from the story that represent events at the beginning, middle, and end.	Student names most of the important events in the story; most of the named events are in sequential order.	Student names all of the important events in the story; all events are given in sequential order.
Problem/ Goal (P/G)	Student mentions the problem or goal of the characters in an indirect manner.	Student specifically mentions the problem/goal of the characters but not in relation to the plot events.	Student specifically mentions the problem/ goal of the characters in relation to the plot events.
Resolution (R)	Student mentions the resolution of the problem/goal in an indirect manner.	Student specifically mentions the resolution of the problem/goal but not in relation to the plot events.	Student specifically mentions the resolution of the problem/goal in relation to plot events.

DATE	TEXT	Level	C	S	P	P/G	R	Total

Story-Specific Retelling Rubric

Outline

Title:

  I. Characters: _____/_____ pts.

   Main Characters: (2 pts. each)

   Supporting Characters: (1 pt. each)

  II. Setting: _____/2 pts.

   Time: (1 pt.)

   Place: (1 pt.)

  III. Events: _____/_____ pts. (1 pt. for each event named)
   Sequence: _____/_____ pts. (1 pt. for each event named in order)

  IV. Problem/Goal: _____/2 pts.

  V. Resolution of Problem/Goal: _____/2 pts.

Total Points: _____/_____ = _____

Story-Specific Retelling Rubric

Sample

Title: *Goldilocks and the Three Bears*

   I. Characters: _____/8 pts.

        Main Characters:
        _____ Goldilocks (2 pts.)   _____ Papa Bear (2 pts.)
        _____ Mama Bear (2 pts.)   _____ Baby Bear (2 pts.)

  II. Setting: _____/2 pts.

        Time: _____ Long ago (1 pt.)

        Place: _____ Forest/Bears' Cottage (1 pt.)

 III. Events: _____/10 pts.
        Sequence: _____/8 pts. (1 pt. for each event named in order)

        _____ She went into cottage uninvited. (initiating event) (2 pts.)
        _____ She tried the chairs—too high, too wide, just right, and broke the "just right" chair. (1 pt.)
        _____ She tried the porridge—too hot, too cold, just right, and ate all the "just right" porridge. (1 pt.)
        _____ She tried the beds—too hard, too soft, just right, and fell asleep in the "just right" bed. (1 pt.)
        _____ Bears came home; found their chairs had been sat in and that Baby Bear's chair was broken. (1 pt.)
        _____ Bears found that someone had been eating their porridge and that Baby Bear's porridge was all gone. (1 pt.)
        _____ Bears found that someone had been sleeping in their beds and that Goldilocks was still asleep in Baby Bear's bed. (1 pt.)
        _____ Goldilocks woke up and was frightened, so she ran away. (2 pts.) (concluding event)

 IV. **Problem/Goal:** _____/2 pts.
        Goldilocks was tired and hungry while she was walking in the woods.

  V. **Resolution of Problem/Goal:** _____/2 pts.
        Goldilocks found the bears' cottage and ate their food and fell asleep.

Total Points: _____/32 = _____%

Comments:

Story-Specific Retelling

Assessment Summary

Student _____ Grade _____

For each assessment, list the date and the level of the text that was read. Put a + in the column for each text element that was acceptable for that retelling. Put a – in the column for each text element that needs additional work. In the "Total %" column, insert the overall percentage earned by the student for that retelling. After listing the retelling results on the summary chart, attach the completed story-specific retelling rubric to the summary sheet.

Key for chart columns:
Characters (C), Setting (S), Events (E), Sequence (SQ), Goal (G), Conclusion (CN)

DATE	TEXT	Level	C	S	E	SQ	CN	Total %

Using Summaries to Assess Recall of Information Text

Background

When assessing students' comprehension of informational (nonfiction) text, teachers use summaries rather than retellings. It is important to distinguish between the two when discussing them with students so that they understand that with informational text, they are not expected to "retell" everything that was read; rather, their task is to summarize what was read into a more concise report so that the relationship of the information in the text is clear. Students will find this process much more difficult than retelling a story because they have much less experience in writing or verbally summarizing informational text than they do in retelling stories.

Grade Levels:	K–12
Materials Needed:	Summary Assessment Rubric and Record Sheet
Data Generated:	A summary rubric will provide data related to the student's memory of what was read in an informational (nonfiction) text.
Data Usage:	Data can be used to identify the student's ability to recall information that was read in nonfiction text. This information can be used to plan subsequent instruction using nonfiction texts.
Directions:	1. When the student has finished reading a nonfiction text (silently), he or she is asked to summarize the text that was read.
	2. The summary can either be written or be oral. It is usually easier to assess a written summary, since you can take your time analyzing the student's work; however, written summaries are much more difficult. Using a written summary may negatively impact the amount of information the student will write. If a student consistently performs poorly when completing a written summary, the teacher should try assessing the student's summarizing skill using an oral summary.
	3. The summary is assessed using the rubric; the score for each assessed summary should be noted on the summary assessment record. This record will allow the teacher to see the student's summarizing strengths/needs at a glance and will also document growth.

Summary Assessment Rubric and Record Sheet

Student _____ Grade _____

Level	Text Structure	Accuracy	Completeness	Paraphrasing
3	Summary reflects the basic text structure of the passage (generalization, cause/effect, problem/solution, enumeration, sequence, compare/contrast).	Information included in the summary is completely accurate.	Information included in the summary reflects the most important information included in the text.	The summary is written in the students' own words.
2	Summary only slightly reflects the basic text structure of the passage.	Information included in the summary is mostly accurate but may indicate a few slight misunderstandings.	Information included in the summary reflects some of the most important information in the text but also includes some less important information.	Summary is mostly written in the student's own words.
1	Summary does not reflect the basic text structure of the passage.	Information included in the summary is mostly accurate but includes a few incorrect facts.	Information included in the summary does not reflect the most important information in the text.	Summary is mostly copied word-for-word from the text and is not in the student's own words.

Assess the student in each of the listed areas. Indicate the score (1–3) for each area in the chart below. In the "Overall Summary" column, indicate the total of all the scores earned for that summary.

Date	Text Level	Overall Summary	Text Structure	Factual Accuracy	Factual Importance	Paraphrasing

Assessing Use of Text Features

Background

Fiction and nonfiction texts do not have the same structure or the same features. In order to effectively read nonfiction texts, students must learn the features to expect in content area textbooks and informational books. Features such as side bars, glossaries, tables of contents, headings, and inset photos are some of the features that students must learn to use effectively in order to comprehend informational text. The Text Features Checklist will assist the teacher in gauging the students' understanding and use of these features.

Grade Levels:	K–12
Materials Needed:	Text Features Checklist
	Writing Implement
Data Generated:	The Text Features Assessment Checklist will provide information relating to the student's understanding and use of text features that are commonly found in informational text.
Data Usage:	Data can be used to identify the text features that students do not use or that they do not use appropriately. This information can be used to plan subsequent individual or group instruction to support students' learning about text features and their use in supporting reading comprehension.
Directions:	1. The teacher should prepare a copy of the Text Features Checklist for each student. It is often helpful to keep the checklists on a clipboard or in a folder so that they are handy.
	2. During content-area instruction using nonfiction texts or during reading instruction when nonfiction texts with text features are the focus of the lesson, the teacher specifically asks students to identify one or more of the listed text features and determines whether the student actually read/used the text feature can effectively utilize the text feature and knows the purpose of the text feature.
	3. Observations made by the teacher are noted on the Text Features Checklist. When the teacher identifies text features that are not used by the students or that the students do not know how to use, instruction should be planned to address those needs.

Text Features Checklist

Name _____ Grade _____

Independent Use

3	Student effectively uses text feature independently.
2	Student sometimes uses text feature independently, usually effectively.
1	Student does not use text feature independently or uses it ineffectively.

Cued Use

3	Student effectively uses text feature when cued by teacher.
2	Student sometimes uses text feature effectively when cued by teacher.
1	Student cannot use text feature effectively, even when cued by teacher.

Understanding

3	Student clearly understands and can explain the purpose of the text feature.
2	Student seems to somewhat understand the purpose of the text feature but may not be able to clearly explain its use.
1	Student does not seem to understand the purpose of the text feature and cannot explain its use.

Date	Text Feature	Independent Use			Cued Use			Understanding		
____	Title	3	2	1	3	2	1	3	2	1
____	Table of Contents	3	2	1	3	2	1	3	2	1
____	Index	3	2	1	3	2	1	3	2	1
____	Glossary	3	2	1	3	2	1	3	2	1
____	Headings/Subtitles	3	2	1	3	2	1	3	2	1
____	Sidebars	3	2	1	3	2	1	3	2	1
____	Pictures/Captions	3	2	1	3	2	1	3	2	1
____	Labeled Diagrams	3	2	1	3	2	1	3	2	1
____	Charts and Graphs	3	2	1	3	2	1	3	2	1
____	Maps	3	2	1	3	2	1	3	2	1
____	Cutaways and Cross-sections	3	2	1	3	2	1	3	2	1
____	Inset Photos	3	2	1	3	2	1	3	2	1

Comments:

Assessment 10.4

Comprehension Strategies Self-Assessment

Background

Determining how much students recall from texts they have read is one clue to their reading comprehension; however, it is also important for teachers to determine *how* students think about the text as they are reading and what strategies they use when they are trying to understand the text. It is often difficult to assess strategy usage because, in general, it cannot often be observed by the teacher. Because of this, self-assessments of comprehension strategy usage are commonly used.

Self-assessments can be administered as interviews for younger students or may be given to older students to complete independently. It is important to be certain that the students can read and understand the questions on the self-assessment before you allow them to complete it on their own. In addition, it is important to stress to students that there are no "right" or "wrong" answers; they should answer the questions honestly and should select answers because they think they are the ones the teacher would want to hear. It is critical that students accurately respond to the questions or the assessment data will not be useful.

Grade Levels:	2–12
Materials Needed:	Comprehension Strategies Self-Assessment
	Writing Implement
Data Generated:	Data will reflect the comprehension strategies that students utilize as they read. Data *does not* show how effectively students actually can *utilize* the strategies.
Data Usage:	Data can be used to determine students' knowledge of a variety of comprehension strategies and their abilities to select appropriate strategies for given reading situations. Based on the data, teachers can plan to introduce comprehension strategies that are unfamiliar to the student, review previously taught strategies that are not being used appropriately, or plan to complete further assessments to determine whether or not the students can effectively utilize the strategies with which they are familiar.

Directions:

1. The assessment should be administered immediately following a reading assignment in which the student reads a text silently and independently. The text should be on the student's instructional reading level so that it is not too easy; if the text is too easy for the student, he or she will not have to use many comprehension strategies while reading.

2. The teacher may administer the assessment as an interview with younger students or with English Language Learners. Older students who are able to understand the questions on their own can complete the assessment individually.

3. Because students approach narrative and expository (informational) text differently, it is important to assess students' comprehension strategy usage while reading both types of text.

Comprehension Strategies Self-Assessment

Name_____ Date_____ Grade_____

Text_____Level_____

Type of Text (circle one):   Informational   Narrative

1. Put a check mark on the line before each of the strategies that you used today to help you understand the text you were reading. You may select as many strategies as you need in order to show all the strategies you used, but do not mark any strategies that you did not actually use today.

   _____ I thought about what I already knew about the topic I was reading about.

   _____ I made predictions about what was going to happen next and then continued to read to find out if my predictions came true.

   _____ When I did not understand what I was reading, I went back to reread a part of the text that I had already read.

   _____ As I was reading, I "made a movie in my head" of what was happening in the text.

   _____ When I came to a part that I did not understand, I asked someone else to help explain it to me.

   _____ When I did not understand what I was reading, I kept reading to see if I could find more information to make the information clearer to me.

   _____ Before I started to read, I looked through the text to read the titles and headings, look at pictures, and get an idea about what the text might be about.

   _____ Before I started to read, I thought about what my goal or purpose was for reading this text.

   _____ As I was reading, I used the pictures to help me figure out words or to help me figure out what was happening in the text.

   _____ As I was reading, I thought about whether the text was making sense to me.

   _____ I drew a diagram or other picture to help me understand the information in the text or what was happening in the text.

   _____ I asked myself questions about what I was reading and made sure I could answer them.

   _____ I thought about what the author's purpose was for writing the text.

2. Put a * next to the strategy you used most today while reading the text.

3. Give an example of *how* you used one of the strategies you used while reading your book today. Try to explain what you were thinking and what you did as you were using the strategy.

_____

_____

_____

_____

_____

_____

_____

_____

_____

_____

_____

_____

4. Were there any other strategies you used today while you were reading? If so, please list them below.

_____

_____

_____

_____

_____

_____

_____

_____

_____

_____

Assessment 10.5

Assessing Comprehension Using Questions

Background

Barrett's Taxonomy (Clymer, 1968) is very similar to Bloom's Taxonomy of the Cognitive Domain, but Barrett relates directly to reading. There are several levels, with each successive level representing a higher level of thinking. Teachers should strive to ask a variety of questions from all levels of Barrett's Taxonomy in order to promote a complete understanding of a text. Students should be encouraged to write their own questions about texts, as well.

Grade Levels:	K–12
Materials Needed:	Barrett's Taxonomy
	Text to be used for assessment
Data Generated:	Data will indicate whether or not students can answer questions about text at each assessed level of Barrett's Taxonomy.
Data Usage:	Data can be used to determine what types of questions students can answer about the texts they have read.
Directions:	1. The teacher should read the text that will form the basis of the assessment.
	2. Questions representing all five levels of Barrett's Taxonomy should be developed. If detailed assessment information for the sublevels is needed, the teacher should focus only on one level for the questions for a particular text, selecting a text that lends itself well to that level. Over the course of the academic year, the teacher should take care to assess the students at each level and sublevel to determine the types of questions that the students can or cannot answer.
	3. Students should read the assessed text silently. Questions can be given in writing or asked orally by the teacher, depending upon the students' reading levels.

Barrett's Taxonomy

1.0 Literal Comprehension

1.1 Recognition
1.1.1 Recognition of Details
1.1.2 Recognition of Main Ideas
1.1.3 Recognition of a Sequence
1.1.4 Recognition of Comparison
1.1.5 Recognition of Cause and Effect Relationships
1.1.6 Recognition of Character Traits

1.2 Recall
1.2.1 Recall of Details
1.2.2 Recall of Main Ideas
1.2.3 Recall of a Sequence
1.2.4 Recall of Comparison
1.2.5 Recall of Cause and Effect Relationships
1.2.6 Recall of Character Traits

2.0 Reorganization

2.1 Classifying
2.2 Outlining
2.3 Summarizing
2.4 Synthesizing

3.0 Inferential Comprehension

3.1 Inferring Supporting Details
3.2 Inferring Main Ideas
3.3 Inferring Sequence
3.4 Inferring Comparisons
3.5 Inferring Cause and Effect Relationships
3.6 Inferring Character Traits
3.7 Predicting Outcomes
3.8 Interpreting Figurative Language

4.0 Evaluation

4.1 Judgments of Reality or Fantasy
4.2 Judgments of Fact or Opinion
4.3 Judgments of Adequacy and Validity
4.4 Judgments of Appropriateness
4.5 Judgments of Worth, Desirability, and Acceptability

5.0 Appreciation

5.1 Emotional Response to the Content
5.2 Identification with Characters or Incidents
5.3 Reactions to the Author's Use of Language
5.4 Imagery

Additional Reading Comprehension Assessments

Online Practice Reading Tests (for LEP students)
http://www.pearsonlongman.com/ae/marketing/sfesl/practicereading.html.

Comprehension Strategy Assessments (Grades 3–4)
http://mvcsd.sharpschool.net/UserFiles/Servers/Server_87286/File/GWallaceELA/
    ComprehensionAssessments_Gr3-4.pdf.

Reading Comprehension Resources
Websites

Reading Comprehension
http://www.bellarmine.edu/Libraries/education_docs/Reutzel_Cooter_Comprehension_TCR_5e_1
    .sflb.ashx.

Reading Comprehension Strategies Chart (Grades 1–3)
http://www.madison.kyschools.us/userfiles/1247/Classes/41049/reading%20comprehension%20
    strategies%20table.pdf?id=561193.

Seven Strategies to Teach Students Text Comprehension
http://www.readingrockets.org/article/3479/.

Books
Cummins, S. (2012). *Close Reading of Informational Texts: Assessment Driven Instruction in Grades
    3–8*. NY: Guilford Press.
Johns, J. & Lenski, S. (2019). *Improving Reading: Strategies, Resources, and Common Core
    Connections*. Dubuque, IA: Kendall Hunt.
Stuart, E & Klein, J. (2012). *Using Art to Teach Reading Comprehension Strategies*. Lanham, MD:
    R. & L. Education.

Videos
Comprehension: Helping English Language Learners Grasp the Full Picture.
http://www.readingrockets.org/webcasts/1005/.

Reading Comprehension
http://oregonliteracypd.uoregon.edu/topic/reading-comprehension.

Reading Comprehension and Strategy Usage

Assessment and Instruction Matrix

Comprehension Strategy	Assessments	Development Activities
Narrative Retelling/Story Elements and Plot	10.1	Story Map
		Story Plot Map
		Story Souvenirs/Story Bits
		Story Pyramid
		Little Book (Narrative)
		Hula Hoop Retelling
		Story Glove
		Baseball Diamond Retelling
		MegaCloze
		Rhythm Instrument Retelling
		Flannel Board Retelling
		Song Retelling
		Story Retelling Beads
		Story Retelling Slide
		Word Plays
Expository Retelling and Expository Summary	10.1, 10.2	Text Pattern Guide
		Text Pattern Graphic Organizers
Using Text Features	10.3	Text Feature Walk
Using Various Strategies	10.4	Monitoring Logs
		Text Coding
		Think Aloud (Modeling)
Visualization		Wordless Picture Book Stories
		Color Words
		Illustrate Word Meanings
		What Book?
		Write the Letter
Using Text Structure		Text Pattern Guide
Rereading/		MegaCloze
Reading Ahead		INSERT/VIP/Think Notes
Predicting/Verifying		Directed Reading-Thinking Activity
		Predictogram
		Anticipation Guide
Using Context Clues		Guess the Covered Word
		Selective Deletion Cloze

Comprehension Strategy	Assessments	Development Activities
Using Prior Knowledge		Text Connections
		Picture Walk
		ABC Brainstorming
		Concept Maps
		Carousel Brainstorming
		Brainstorming L-G-L
		KWL and Variations
		Semantic/Story Impressions
		Predictogram
		Anticipation Guide
		Talking Drawings
		Think-Pair-Share and Turn and Talk
		THIEVES
Using Picture Clues		Add a Page
		Unlikely Pairs
		Story Interpretation
		Write the Story of the Picture
		Story Tableau
		Wordless Picture Book Stories
Using Graphic		Text Pattern Graphic Organizers
Organizers		Story Plot Map
Asking/Answering Questions	10.4, 10.5	Question-Answer-Relationships
About Text		SQ3R/SQ4R
		ACES
		Fact-Question-Response (FQR) Chart
		IBET (Text-Based Inferences)
		Sentence Starters (Text Dependent Questions)

Chapter Activities

1. Using the directions provided in this chapter, develop a story-specific retelling assessment for a narrative text.
2. Select an expository text suitable for students who are reading on a fourth-grade instructional reading level. Write one question for each level and sublevel of Barrett's Taxonomy.
3. Use the story-specific retelling rubric on p. 196 to assess Rudy's retelling of Goldilocks and the Three Bears:

Goldilocks went walking in the woods. She found a house, and since she was tired and hungry, she went in. She found a chair to sit in, but it was too big. The next one was not right either. The smallest one was just right, but when she sat in it, the chair got broken. Then she went into the kitchen to find some lunch. The first bowl of food was too hot, and the next one was too cold, but the last one was just right, so she ate it all up. Then she was tired and wanted to take a nap. She went upstairs and checked the beds. The big one was too hard, the middle one was too soft, but the baby one was just right, so she fell asleep. Then the three bears came home, and they found the broken chairs. When they went to eat lunch, the baby's food was all gone. Then they went upstairs and found her sleeping in the baby's bed! Then she woke up and was afraid of the bears, so she ran away home. The End.

PART II

Instructional Strategies

ABC Brainstorming

Purpose

The purposes of an ABC brainstorming activity are to:

- Activate and assess students' prior knowledge about the topic(s) of a book that you are going to be reading or a lesson you are going to teach.
- Motivate students and build interest in the book or topic.
- Identify vocabulary that students know or may need to learn.

Types of Text

ABC brainstorming can be used with both nonfiction and fiction.

Steps

Preparation

1. Identify the main topic of the text or lesson (e.g., trees).
2. For each letter of the alphabet, try to identify a word related to the topic that begins with that letter. You should do this in advance so that you can provide support to the students if they get "stuck" on a particular letter.

Implementation

1. Introduce the book/topic to the students.
2. Have the students work individually to try to identify as many words related to the topic as they can.
3. After the students have tried the activity individually, put them with a partner to add to their lists.
4. Make a class list or word wall of the words identified by the students. While the students are working and sharing their words, listen to their conversations to identify which students have insufficient prior knowledge of the topic and will benefit from background-building activities, as well as which students have incorrect prior knowledge that needs to be corrected.
5. As the students read the text or you complete the lesson, point to the identified words on the chart/word wall and add additional words.

Alternative Activities

Use the ABC Brainstorm as an Assessment

The ABC brainstorm can also be used as an assessment. Have the students complete the ABC word list activity after they finish reading or after you have finished teaching a lesson in order to give you insight as to what the students remember from the text/lesson.

Add a Summary Paragraph

Have students write a sentence or a paragraph about the topic, using some of the words they brainstormed for the activity.

ABC Brainstorming

A	**N**
B	**O**
C	**P**
D	**Q**
E	**R**
F	**S**
G	**T**
H	**U**
I	**V**
J	**W**
K	**X**
L	**Y**
M	**Z**

ACES

The ACES (answer, citations, explanations/elaboration, and summary) instructional strategy was first described by Rogowski and Elliott in 2007.

Purpose

The purpose of the ACES instructional strategy is to:

- Provide students with a mnemonic to help them write adequate responses to text-dependent question.

Types of Text

ACES can be used with any type of text but works particularly well with expository text.

Steps

Preparation

1. Preparing an ACES anchor chart or bookmark for the students' reference will help them remember the mnemonic more quickly.
2. Identify a text to use to model ACES with the students, and prepare it so that each member of the group has a copy of the text. You could also display it on a chart or SmartBoard so that everyone can see it.
3. Prepare a list of five questions based on the text to use for practice with the students.
4. Write a sample answer for two of the questions to use for practice with the students.

Implementation

1. Display the ACES anchor chart, and review the mnemonic with the students:
   A = Answer the Question
   C = Cite the Text
   E = Explain or elaborate on the text citation
   S = Summarize your conclusion
2. Display one of the questions for the sample text and the written answer. Point out each of the parts of the answer for the students. Use a highlighter or marker to label the answer (A), citations (C), explanations/elaborations (E), and summary (S).

3. Give the students a second question and its written answer. Have them work in pairs to label the parts of the answer as you did in Step 2. Review their responses when everyone has finished.

4. Provide the students with the remaining three questions you have prepared. For each question, ask them to write their answer and then label the parts of the answer.

5. Review the answers and labels with the group when everyone has finished.

Extension

When the students have mastered the ACES process, introduce "ACES Squared." In this version of the mnemonic, students are asked to come up with two text citations and two explanations/elaborations.

Add-a-Page

In the add-a-page instructional strategy, students analyze and study a picture book to identify choices made by the author and illustrator of the book. Students then create a new page to add somewhere within the text, imitating the author's writing style (vocabulary, tone, rhythm, etc.) and the presentation choices (font, media, color, placement of font on page, etc.) as closely as possible.

Purpose

The purposes of the add-a-page instructional strategy are to:

- Develop students' visual literacy skills.
- Encourage students to "read like writers" by stepping into the author's shoes to identify decisions the author made about word choice, presentation, and other writing traits.
- Help students learn to use mentor texts to teach them about writing.
- Encourage students to look closely at illustrations, fonts, colors, media, and other presentation aspects of texts.

Types of Text

The add-a-page strategy is designed to be used with any text that includes images and text. Picture books work especially well for this strategy, regardless of the age/grade level of the students.

Implementation

1. Show students some sample pages that were created to add to books with which they are familiar.
2. Point out the similarities in writing style and visual presentation between the original book and the added page.
3. If students are not catching on to the idea, you may model the creation of a page to add to a book, demonstrating how to analyze the page to determine the choices made by the author and illustrator.
4. Students select a picture book, read it, and create a page to add to the book. Their task is to create a page that fits seamlessly into the story.
5. Have students share their books and added pages, explaining the choices they made for the new page.

Technology Connections

The text for added pages should be printed using a computer, as this will mostly permit students to most closely replicate the font styles utilized in the majority of picture books.

© photographer/Shutterstock.com

Alliterative Books

Purpose

The purpose of using alliterative books with students is to help them develop phonemic awareness skills. In particular, alliterative books support students in listening for and identifying initial sounds in words.

Types of Text

Alliterative books can be made using any text type. Most published alliterative books are fiction.

Steps

Preparation

1. Identify an alliterative text that highlights the target sound for the lesson.
2. Keep track of the initial sounds that have been introduced and used for this activity so that you can be sure to include as many different initial sounds as possible throughout the school year.

Implementation

1. Read the text to the students.
2. Ask the students if they heard a particular sound repeated often in the text.
3. Read the text again, asking the students to raise their hands or give you a thumbs-up if they hear the target sound. Since some books repeat the sound numerous times per page, you may want to limit this part of the activity to just a few pages of the text.
4. Ask the students to dictate sentences to you that include the target sound. Since it is the sound that is the focus of the lesson, not spelling, it's okay if the sound is spelled using a variety of patterns. For example, "phone" and "fox" begin with the /f/ sound, so both would be acceptable in a story focusing on the /f/ sound.
5. Give each student a sentence to illustrate. Combine them into an alliterative book that focuses on the target sound.

Extension

Once students have developed phonemic awareness, this activity can be used to reinforce sound/symbol correspondences. Give students letter cards to hold up when they hear a particular sound in the text. Focus on specific spelling patterns along with the sound patterns when you develop the alliterative books.

Recommended Alliterative Texts

Atwood, Margaret	*Princess Prunella and the Purple Peanut*
Breen, Steve	*Woodpecker Wants a Waffle*
Carle, Eric	*"Slowly, Slowly, Slowly," said the Sloth*
Courtney, Suzanne Gene	*Florence Flies Alone*
Crimi, Carolyn	*Tessa's Tip-Tapping Toes*
Edwards, Pamela Duncan	*Clara Caterpillar*
	Four Famished Foxes and Fosdyke
	Princess Pigtoria and the Pea
	Rosie's Roses
	Some Smug Slug
	The Worrywarts
Heck, Ed	*Many Marvelous Monsters*
Henkes, Kevin	*Lilly's Purple Plastic Purse*
	Wemberley Worried
Nichols, Travis	*Betty's Burgled Bakery*
Palatini, Margie	*Bedhead*
Seeger, Laura Vaccaro	*Walter Was Worried*
Sierra, Judy	*Counting Crocodiles*
Smith, Maggie	*Pigs in Pajamas*
Stevens, Janet	*The Great Fuzzy Frenzy*
Wood, Audrey	*Silly Sally*

Alphabet Books/Personalized Alphabet Books

Alphabet books are published books that present each letter of the alphabet. Generally, they also show pictures of items that begin with the sound(s) of each letter. Many alphabet books are coordinated around a particular topic. Personalized alphabet books are made by children. They are "personalized" because the students can select the overall topic, words, and images they want to include in their own book.

Purpose

Alphabet books can be used to introduce the letters of the alphabet and to help students learn sound/symbol correspondences.

Types of Text

Alphabet books can be based on fictional stories and characters or may be informational text.

Steps

Preparation

The teacher should introduce a selection of alphabet books to the students and read them aloud frequently. These books can be used for guides as the students create their own personalized alphabet books. The teacher should be careful to select alphabet books that are age-appropriate. There are many fabulous alphabet books that are actually written for older students to learn vocabulary in the content areas. Be sure to limit choices to those that are geared toward emergent learners.

Implementation

1. After students are familiar with the layout of alphabet books (one letter per page in most cases), they can begin to assemble their own books.
2. As each letter is learned, students should create a page for that letter. You may have the students create their books around a similar theme or topic or allow each student to select his or her own theme. For example, the entire class may make animal alphabet books, food alphabet books, or name alphabet books. Each page should contain the uppercase and lowercase letter and pictures of objects beginning with that letter.

3. When the students have learned each letter of the alphabet and have created a page for each letter, the pages can be compiled into a book. Students may read their books to the class or keep them for reference.

Extensions

1. Students can add additional images or words to their alphabet books as they learn them.
2. In pairs, students can read their books to a partner.

Technology Connections

1. If students have access to a computer and printer, they can create their alphabet books using a Word processing program and clip art.
2. Using the books *Alphabet City* and *Alphabet School* as guides, have the students look for letters in the environment. Use digital cameras to photograph the letters to create a book. This activity builds visual literacy while it reinforces letter identification.

Recommended Alphabet Books

American Museum of Natural History	*ABC Animals*
Bayer, Jane E.	*A My Name Is Alice*
Boynton, Sandra	*A to Z*
Carle, Eric	*Eric Carle's ABC*
Ehlert, Lois	*Eating the Alphabet*
Fleming, Denise	*Alphabet under Construction*
Johnson, Stephen	*Alphabet City*
Johnson, Stephen	*Alphabet School*
Kalman, Marie	*What Pete Ate from A to Z*
Kitamura, Satoshi	*From Acorn to Zoo*
Marzollo, Jean	*I Spy Little Letters*
Metropolitan Museum of Art	*My First ABC*
Micklethwait, Lucy	*I Spy: An Alphabet in Art*
Pallotta, Jerry	All of his books are wonderful
Vamos, Samantha	*Alphabet Trucks*
Werner, Sharon	*Alphabeasties*

Alphabet Scavenger Hunt

An alphabet scavenger hunt engages students at the emergent literacy stage in actively seeking letters in the print environment around them.

Purpose

The purpose of an alphabet scavenger hunt is to support students' recognition of letters.

Types of Text

The alphabet scavenger hunt activity can be completed using a wide variety of texts, including books, magazines, posters, signs, labels, and any other items containing print.

Steps

Preparation

1. Prepare a scavenger hunt list for each student or for each student pair if you prefer to have students working with a partner. The list should include five to ten target letters for the students to locate in the classroom.
2. Include a place for the students to write the letter or place a check mark for each time they find the correct letter. The scavenger hunt list might look something like this:

Name: _____

A _____ _____ _____ _____

F _____ _____ _____ _____

M _____ _____ _____ _____

R _____ _____ _____ _____

T _____ _____ _____ _____

Implementation

1. Model the process of completing the letter list. Students should be shown how to look for each letter in the print contained in the classroom. When they find the correct letter, they either write the letter on the line or put a check or X on the line, depending upon which approach you would like to use for the activity.

2. Once the students understand how to complete the activity, give them time to look for the letters. This may also be done as an independent learning center activity once the students are familiar with the process.

Alternatives

The alphabet scavenger hunt can be modified to keep the activity engaging. Here are some possibilities:

- Have the students hunt for the letters in magazines or discarded books. They can then cut out the letters that they find and glue them on the page.
- Assign the activity for homework and have the students hunt for alphabet letters at home.
- Extend the activity to outside the classroom by taking the students for a walk around the school or community, looking for letters.
- Give the students a clipboard for their letter charts to make it easier for them to write.
- Purchase some inexpensive and funky sunglasses. Introduce them to the students as "Alphabet Specs," and have them wear these as they hunt for letters.

© photographer/Shutterstock.com

Alphabet Thief

Alphabet thief is an instructional strategy that engages students in a fun game designed to help them learn letters of the alphabet.

Purpose

Alphabet thief supports students' learning of the alphabet in order. In addition, students will identify individual letters of the alphabet.

Steps

Preparation

1. Prepare letter cards or cut-out letters of the alphabet for use in the game. Magnetic letters can also be used.
2. Hang the letters of the alphabet on the whiteboard for a class or group activity. For a small group or an individual, lay out the letters on a table or on the floor.
3. Students should already have been introduced to the alphabet and have some proficiency in saying it.

Implementation

1. Ask the students what a "thief" is. If they aren't sure, explain that a thief is someone who takes something that doesn't belong to them.
2. Ask the students to close their eyes.
3. Take away one of the letters.
4. When students open their eyes, ask them to identify the letter that was "stolen" by the alphabet thief. Have the students give you a thumbs-up if they know which letter was stolen. Wait until all or most of the students have identified the letter before continuing.
5. Starting with *A*, say the alphabet as you point to each of the letters. Ask the students to say it with you. When you come to the missing letter, stop and ask which letter comes next.
6. Repeat the process several times.

Alternative Activities

- Give the students whiteboards and erasable markers, and ask them to write the letter that is missing. When you get to that letter in the alphabet, ask them to turn their boards around and hold them up so you can see who correctly identified the missing letter.
- If students cannot write the letters but can identify them on sight, provide each student with a set of letter cards. They can hold up the missing letter using a letter card.
- Have the students take turns being the alphabet thief. Be sure to give each student in the group a turn.
- After the students are rather proficient with the alphabet, remove most of the letters and only give them a set of four to five letters at a time, such as *LMNOP*. Remove one of the letters in the smaller segment of the alphabet.

Alphabet Books

While many alphabet books stress words that begin with a particular letter, some focus more on the order of the letters. These books can be used to introduce or reinforce the alphabet thief activity. Some excellent choices are as follows:

Kontis, Alethea	*Alpha Oops! The Day Z Went First*
MacCuish, Al	*Operation Alphabet*
Martin, Bill and Archambault, John	*Chicka-Chicka-Boom-Boom*
Wood, Audrey	*Alphabet Adventure*
Wood, Audrey	*Alphabet Mystery*

© photographer/Shutterstock.com

Analogic Phonics

Analogic phonics is one approach for teaching phonics. It is very useful for students who are in the full alphabetic phase of word identification.

Purpose

The purpose of analogic phonics is to help students learn to look for chunks or patterns in words. Students use analogies to compare one word with another, looking for parts they recognize. For example, if students know the word "take," help them identify the "take" in the word "mistake" as a chunk they recognize.

Steps

Preparation

1. Prior to reading a text, look through it to identify words that lend themselves to analogic phonics. These words should have "little words" in the "big word."
2. To introduce the idea, it's helpful to prepare some word cards that show the words you'll be comparing. Underline the "little word" in the big word or print it in a different color to make it stand out.

Implementation

1. Introduce the idea of finding the "little word in the big word" to the students.
2. Model the process using several words.
3. Have students practice identifying the little words in the big words using three or four words from the text you are planning to read.
4. Have the students read the text.
5. After reading the text, have the students go back to identify some words that they identified using the "little words in a big word" strategy.

Anticipation and Anticipation/ Reaction Guides

Anticipation guides are completed prior to reading to assist students in using their prior knowledge. It also assists students in learning the cognitive process of anticipating when reading. If the activity also includes a postreading component, it is called an anticipation/reaction guide.

Purpose

As a prereading instructional strategy, the purposes of using an anticipation guide are to:

- Activate and assess students' prior knowledge about the topic(s) of a text that you are going to be reading or a lesson you will be teaching.
- Motivate students and build interest in the text or lesson.
- Provide the teacher with an opportunity to identify and correct misinformation about a topic prior to reading.
- Support students' use of the cognitive process of anticipating when reading, and, when checked after reading, they assist students in learning to verify their predictions (anticipation/reaction guide).
- Model the process of predicting and asking questions prior to reading expository text.
- Model the process of verifying predictions following reading.

Types of Text

Anticipation guides can be used with both fiction and nonfiction text.

Steps

Preparation

1. Read through the text.
2. Write four to six statements about the text that can be answered "yes" or "no."
3. Use the blank template for the anticipation guide to format the questions for students' use.

Implementation

1. When you first introduce anticipation guides to your students, you should model the process of completing the guide. You should complete the anticipation guide as the students watch. As you complete it, think aloud through the process so the students can hear what you are thinking. Also, be sure to model the postreading process of verifying your predictions.

2. After students have learned how to complete anticipation guides, you can allow them to complete the guides independently.

3. Introduce the text, and then have the students complete the anticipation guide.

4. After the students read the assigned text, have them revisit their predictions on the anticipation guide and verify whether or not they were correct.

5. Options for anticipation guides:
   a. Use lists of "yes" and "no" questions.
   b. Use lists of facts, and have the students identify them as "true" or "false."
   c. Use lists of characteristics, and have the students identify how they will relate to the text. For example, in a book about the Civil War, the students might predict whether a "Yank" relates to the North or South.
   d. Add a third column to the anticipation guide for the verification stage. Students may indicate if their predictions were correct (yes/no) or you may have them put the page number from the text that verifies their prediction.

Sample Anticipation/Reaction Guides

Me and Uncle Romie

Read each question about the book *Me and Uncle Romie* by Claire Hartfield. Choose *yes* or *no* for each question. Mark your answers in the Before Reading column.

Before Reading			After Reading	
Yes	No	1. Uncle Romie is an artist.	Yes	No
Yes	No	2. This is a true story.	Yes	No
Yes	No	3. Uncle Romie lives in the city.	Yes	No
Yes	No	4. Uncle Romie lives in the country.	Yes	No
Yes	No	5. Harlem is part of New York City.	Yes	No
Yes	No	6. A collage is a type of painting.	Yes	No

After you have finished reading the book *Me and Uncle Romie*, answer each question again in the After Reading column.

Check your answers in the book. Put a star * next to the questions you got correct after reading.

Leonardo daVinci
by Mary Pope Osborne

Before Reading			After Reading	
Agree	Disagree		Agree	Disagree
_____	_____	1. Leonardo daVinci was a painter.	_____	_____
_____	_____	2. Leonardo daVinci was a scientist.	_____	_____
_____	_____	3. Leonardo daVinci was an inventor.	_____	_____
_____	_____	4. Leonardo daVinci invented the first airplane.	_____	_____
_____	_____	5. Leonardo daVinci lived in Italy his whole life.	_____	_____

Antiphonal Reading

Antiphonal reading occurs when students read parts, similar to singing a round. The reading goes back and forth between the voices, with some choral reading thrown in as well. Antiphonal reading is excellent for developing appropriate rate, expression, stress/inflection (supra-segmental phonemes), and phrasing.

Steps

Preparation

1. Select an appropriate text that has been written for more than one voice, or create one of your own.
2. Duplicate the parts so that each student has a text to read. Highlight the part that is going to be read to alleviate students' problems with losing their place.

Implementation

1. Explain to the students how the reading will work, with the voices taking turns reading or reading together, depending upon the layout of the text on the script.
2. You may want to read along with one part and then switch to the other part during the second reading.

Suggested Texts for Antiphonal Reading

Fleischman, Paul	*Big Talk: Poems for Four Voices.*
Fleischman, Paul	*I Am Phoenix: Poems for Two Voices.*
Fleischman, Paul	*Joyful Noise: Poems for Two Voices.*
Hoberman, Mary Ann	*You Read to Me, I'll Read to You: Very Short Stories to Read Together.*
Hoberman, Mary Ann	*You Read to Me, I'll Read to You: Very Short Fairy Tales to Read Together.*
Pappas, Theoni	*Math Talk: Mathematical Ideas in Poems for Two Voices.*

Baseball Diamond Retelling

Purpose

The purposes of the baseball diamond retelling instructional strategy are to:

- Motivate students to participate in story retellings.
- Provide a framework to assist students in retelling a story by reminding them of the story events and sequence.
- Incorporate kinesthetic activities into the retelling process.
- Support students' summarizing of stories.

Types of Text

The baseball diamond retelling instructional strategy can be done with any narrative text. It is an excellent activity to use to introduce the idea of summarizing a text or as practice in summarizing for a postreading activity.

Steps

Preparation

1. Purchase or create four bases to lay out in your classroom in the traditional baseball diamond pattern. Label them *first base, second base, third base*, and *home*.
2. You may also prepare paper baseball diamonds for students to use on their own. Students may keep these at their desks to use as a scaffold for retelling, or you may have them write on them to organize a written retelling. A diagram of the baseball diamond can also be made into an anchor chart for student reference during subsequent retelling activities.

Implementation

1. Demonstrate to the students that they can use the baseball diamond to remind themselves of the story events and the sequence of the events in the story.
2. After reading a story, have the students retell it by moving to the first base to tell the beginning of the story, moving to second base to tell the middle of the story, and moving to third base to tell the end of the story. Then have them "bring the retell home" by moving to home plate and retelling the entire story in one or two summary sentences.

Being the Words

Purpose

The purpose of the instructional strategy being the words is to develop emergent literacy concepts in an engaging manner.

- Being the words will help students learn left-to-right progression.
- The activity will reinforce the emergent literacy concept of "concept of word," so that the students learn where one word starts and ends.
- Being the words reinforces one-to-one correspondence so students know that there is one word read for each word in the text.

Steps

Preparation

1. Select several five- to seven-word sentences from a story that has recently been read by to the students so that they are familiar with the text. The repeated words from a predictable text is an excellent choice.
2. Write the sentence on a sentence strip.

Implementation

1. Read the predictable text with the students, and have them chime in when they can.
2. Show a sentence strip, and read it to the students, having them repeat it after you. Point out that there are spaces between the words.
3. Give each student a pair of scissors, and have them cut the sentence strip apart between each word. For example, the sentence, "Joseph had a little overcoat" would be cut into five segments, each containing one word.
4. Have the students mix up the words and then reassemble them using a noncut sentence strip as a guide. Ask the students to read the sentence with you, pointing at each word as it is said.
5. Hang a sentence strip on the whiteboard. Give each student a word from the sentence and have them form themselves into the sentence by "being the words" and standing in the correct order. Have each student say his or her word aloud as the sentence is read by the group.

Big Books with Pointers/Shared Reading

Big books are large books designed to be used with a group of students. Because they are large, they are easy for all the students to see.

Purpose

Big Books can be used to reinforce several different emergent literacy and early literacy skills. These include the following:

- Return Sweep: The big book can be used to demonstrate the return sweep, which must be made when students reach the end of a line and must sweep their eyes down to the beginning of the next sentence.
- One-to-One Matching: A big book can be used to demonstrate one-to-one correspondence so that students learn that there is one word said for each word in the text.
- Sight Words: Big books can be used with pointers or frames to help students learn to identify common sight words.
- Letter Identification: Big books and frames or pointers can also be used to support letter identification. After reading the book to the students, ask them to come up to point to or frame a particular letter or a letter that makes a particular sound.
- Students at the prephonemic stage in spelling will benefit from participation in big book activities. Frames and pointers can be used to identify words that start with specific letters or sounds.

Types of Text

Most big books are narrative text, but there are some that are informational text. Either type of text can be used for these activities, as the focus is on the words rather than the actual content of the text.

Frames and Pointers

Frames and pointers for these activities can be purchased, but they are also easy and inexpensive to make. Here are some ideas for creating them yourself.

Frames

- Purchase inexpensive fly swatters at a dollar store. Use scissors or a craft knife to cut out a rectangle in the center of the swatter to use as the frame. Be sure to make several different size openings for use with different size words.
- Cut various-sized holes in index cards, and use them as frames.

Pointers

- A wide variety of pointers can be purchased. After Halloween, purchase wands (fairy god mother wands, wizard wands, etc.) when they are on clearance to use as pointers.
- Use straws or popsicle sticks as the base for homemade pointers. Be creative with the tops to reflect holidays or seasons. For example, use cotton balls to make a snowflake or construction paper to make flowers. Glue these to the end of the bases to make pointers. Cut-out stars can be used to make them into homemade wands.
- Buy inexpensive flashlights to use as pointers. Turn out the lights, and have the students shine the light on the target word or letter.
- Glue a feather to the end of a base to make a special pointer. Ask the students to "tickle" the target word or letter.
- Decorate tongue depressors, and have students glue a googly-eye at the end of each one. Have them use these to "put their eye on" a particular letter or word. You can be creative or have them make these into one-eyed "minions" such as those in the "Despicable Me" movies.

Book Clubs

Oprah Winfrey made book clubs very popular. Use the same idea in your classroom to encourage students to talk about books.

Purpose

The purpose of book clubs is to motivate students to read and to encourage them to discuss the books they have read with their peers. Students can develop deeper understanding as they articulate and defend their opinions.

Types of Text

Book clubs can be used with any type of text, although students generally find it easier to discuss narrative texts or informational texts that have a narrative format, such as those based on historical events.

Steps

1. Students may choose their own books, or you may provide a narrow selection and provide limited choices. Limiting their choices allows you to control text difficulty or content. If your goal is to encourage motivation to read, allowing the students to choose their own texts is preferable.
2. You may choose several books on the same topic or set during the same time period as a way to build prior knowledge for future lessons in social studies, history, or science.
3. Similar to a literature circle, students read the book according to a schedule they establish themselves and then meet to discuss it. Unlike a literature circle, there are no roles or assigned tasks for the students to complete following their reading.
4. When students have finished reading, you may choose to have them share their books with the class or complete an activity to extend their understanding of the book. These should not be "book reports" in the traditional sense but should encourage the students to make personal connections with the text.

Brainstorming-List-Group-Label

The brainstorming-list-group-label instructional strategy was developed by Hilda Taba in 1967.

Purpose

The purposes of the brainstorming-list-group-label (BLGL) activity are to:

- Activate and assess students' prior knowledge about the topic(s) of a book that you are going to be reading or a lesson that you are going to teach.
- Motivate students and build interest in the book or topic.
- Identify vocabulary that students know or may need to learn.
- Determine whether students have an understanding of the relationships among the words/concepts generated about the topic.

Types of Text

Brainstorming-list-group-label can be used with both nonfiction and fiction. It works particularly well with nonfiction text.

Steps

Preparation

1. Identify the main topic of the text or lesson (e.g., England)
2. Generate a list of vocabulary terms related to the topic or from the text that will be read, which you think are important for the students to know.
3. Write your words on sticky notes or individual index cards.

Implementation

1. Introduce the book/topic to the students.
2. Brainstorming: Give each student two to four sticky notes or index cards. Tell them to write one word that relates to the topic on each card/note.
3. List: Have the students bring their sticky notes/index cards to the board. If you are using index cards, you will need a pocket chart to hold the words. If you use sticky notes, the students may stick the note to the chalkboard or chart.

4. Remove all the duplicate words so that there is only one of each word on the board/chart. Read through the words orally with the students.

5. Group: In groups, have the students discuss the words and determine logical groups for them. For example, in a BLGL about trees, the groups might be types of trees, products from trees, parts of trees, uses for trees, and so on.

6. Label: Discuss the ideas for the groupings, and determine which groups the class will use. Write the headings (labels) on the board or sentence strip (if you are using a pocket chart), and have the students assist you in sorting the words into the correct categories. As you sort each word, talk about what the word means and why it belongs in that particular category.

7. Add any words that you thought of beforehand that were not thought of by the students. Discuss the words and make sure the students understand what they mean and how they relate to the topic.

Follow-up Ideas

Word Wall

Use the word cards/sticky notes as the basis of a word wall, to which you can add additional words as you read the text or complete the lesson/unit.

Writing Predictions

Have the students use the sticky notes/word cards to write a prediction about what the text might be about.

Carousel Brainstorming

Purpose

The purposes of a carousel brainstorming activity are to:

- Activate and assess students' prior knowledge about the topic(s) of a book that you are going to read or a lesson you are going to teach.
- Motivate students and build interest in the book or topic.

Types of Text

The carousel brainstorming instructional strategy can be used with nonfiction and with fiction, but it works especially well with nonfiction text.

Steps

Preparation and Implementation

1. Divide the students into small groups of three to four.
2. Give each group a piece of chart paper with the topic written at the top and a marker. Each group should have a different color marker so that you can see which groups have added which pieces of information to the chart.
3. Explain to the students that they will have two minutes to write down everything that they can think of related to the topic written at the top of the page. One student in each group will do the writing.
4. After the students have brainstormed for two minutes, sound a buzzer or use another signal for them to stop. Explain that they will pass the chart to the team on their right. For the second round, students will have two minutes to
   a. read over the chart they have been given,
   b. check the information that is already written,
   c. correct any information they believe is incorrect,
   d. add to information that is already there, and
   e. add new information about the topic that is not yet on the chart.
5. Call time at the end of the second round, and have the students again pass their chart to the team on their right. For rounds three and four, students will repeat the same process, only they will have just one minute and thirty seconds to work on the charts. If you have five or six groups in the class, repeat the process again for as many rounds as you need, decreasing the work time to one minute per group.

6. When the groups receive their original chart back, they should read over the entire chart, paying particular attention to their original brainstorming. Were corrections made to what they wrote? Did anyone elaborate on their original comments? This part of the activity is critical in order to have the students recognize incomplete or incorrect prior knowledge. Having the students read over the entire chart helps to build prior knowledge or activate prior knowledge that may have been forgotten.

Choral Reading

Choral reading is especially effective for building phrasing, appropriate rate, and expression in oral reading fluency. It also provides support to less-able readers, as they are reading along with a group.

Steps

Preparation

1. Select text that lends itself to being read aloud.
2. Read through the text yourself several times so that you can read it perfectly, with appropriate expression and phrasing. Remember, you are going to be the model for the students to follow.

Implementation

1. Read the text aloud to the students once, as they follow along in their copies of the text. This builds familiarity with vocabulary and gives the students a chance to listen to your phrasing and expression.
2. Begin the reading again, reading at a normal rate, using good expression and appropriate phrasing. The students should read along with you. Your voice should be loud enough that it can be heard above the students' voices.
3. Stress to the students that they should try to make their reading sound as much like yours as possible.

Clustering Activities

Purpose

The purposes of the clustering instructional strategy are to:

- Build students' oral reading fluency.
- Promote and encourage reading with syntactically appropriate phrasing.

Types of Text

Clustering activities can be done with any text. All activities for developing reading fluency should be based on texts at the student's instructional or independent reading level. Ideally, the students should have already read the text silently, in its entirety, before it is used for fluency activities.

Steps

Preparation

1. Select a short passage from an appropriate text.
2. Read through it yourself several times so that you can read it aloud fluently, paying particular attention to syntactically correct phrasing.
3. Write the text on a chart or transparency.

Implementation

1. Show the students the text sample chart/transparency, and read it aloud to them, providing an excellent model of fluent reading.
2. Discuss how some words "go together." Tell students that authors use signals in the text to help the reader know when to pause. Look for the text signals, such as commas and other punctuations, in the sample text, and discuss what message the author is sending to the reader by using those signals.
3. Circle the clusters of words that "go together." Show students that there is not always a text signal, but they should use them when they can.
4. Have the students practice reading the marked text chorally and then in pairs.
5. Use the marked text for repeated reading practice for several days. By the time the students have read the marked text several times, you will see that they are beginning to pause between the phrases.
6. Give the students the original, unmarked text, and have them listen to how they are now reading in appropriate phrases.

Collecting Words

Purpose

The purposes of the collecting words instructional strategy are to:

- Encourage students to apply their knowledge of morphemes to their everyday reading.
- Encourage students to use analogy when identifying unknown words (looking for chunks of words that they recognize).
- Encourage students to use their knowledge of the meanings of morphemes to try to identify words that have the same morphemes.

Types of Text

The collecting words instructional strategy can be used with either fiction or nonfiction text.

Steps

Preparation

1. Teach students the meaning of a target morpheme, such as the prefix *un*, meaning *not*.
2. Look for several examples of words that have the un prefix in books, newspapers, magazines, and other texts.

Implementation

1. Explain to the students that you want them to be word detectives. Their job is to hunt for the target morpheme (*un-*, in our example) and to bring in as many examples of words that have the prefix *un-* as they can find.
2. Show the students your example *un-* words. Read the sentence in which the *un-* words are found and discuss the meaning of each of the words. Stress that in each example, *un-* means "not."
3. Write each of the *un-* words you found on index cards or word strips, and use them to begin an *un-* word wall.
4. As the students find and bring in *un-* words to share, have each student share his or her "find" with the class by reading the sentence in which the word was found and discussing the meaning of the word with the class. Provide assistance, as needed, if there are other words in the sentence that are difficult to read. Stress again that in each word, *un-* means "not."

5. Have each student prepare a word strip or index card for each of the words and add them to the word wall.

6. If a student brings in a word that has the correct spelling but not the correct meaning of *un* (for example, *un* in the word "under"), stress that in that word, the *un* is not a prefix and does not mean "not." You might want to have a separate word wall for "other words with *un*" so that all words that are brought in will be displayed.

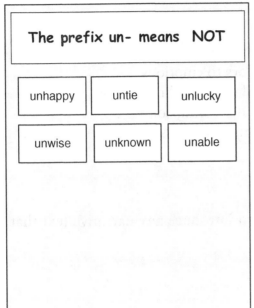
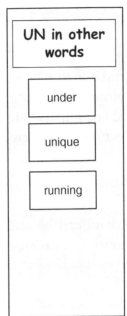

Color Words

Purpose

The purposes of the color words instructional strategy are to:

- Encourage students to relate colors to emotions.
- Support development of vocabulary related to color words and to encourage students to use specific vocabulary when discussing colors.
- Provide opportunities for students to express themselves creatively.

Types of Text

The color words activity can be used to introduce any narrative text that models the use of color to portray emotions in the story.

Steps

Preparation

1. Create sets of color cards to use for the activity. Each group will need a set of cards.
2. Read through a book that uses colors to portray emotions so that you are prepared to read it fluently for the students.

Implementation

1. Give each small group of students a set of color cards. Allow them to talk about the colors for a short time—choosing their favorite/least favorite colors, and so on.
2. Throughout the activity, emphasize appropriate color-related vocabulary. For example, instead of "blue," a color might be turquoise, azure, midnight, navy, and so on.
3. You may want to have the students arrange the color cards in a gradient from the lightest to the darkest of each color to introduce the idea of semantic gradients.
4. After the students are familiar with the cards and some specific color words, ask them to select the color card that is the
   * happiest   *scariest   *warmest
   * saddest   *loneliest   *meanest
   * coldest   *funniest   *sweetest

5. Read the selected book aloud for the students, taking more time than usual to show the illustrations.

6. After reading the story once, go back through the book and discuss the colors on each page. Have the students explain how the colors make them feel and how that matches with the events occurring at that point in the story.

Extensions

1. Put the color cards in a bag. Each student selects three cards from the bag.

2. Have the students write a word that each color card brings to their mind.

3. Students then use the three cards/words to write a story—the first card is the beginning of the story; the second card, the middle of the story; and the third card is the end of the story.

Color Cards

Large paint sample cards or strips from the hardware store can be cut apart to make color cards. Wallpaper or construction paper can also be used, but there will be a more limited array of colors available.

Concept Maps

Concept maps are graphic organizers that are used to show the relationships among concepts and the vocabulary words that represent those concepts. They were first developed by Novak in 1972.

Purpose

As a prereading instructional strategy, the purposes of using a concept map are to:

- Activate and assess students' prior knowledge about the topic(s) of a text that you are going to be reading or a lesson you will be teaching.
- Motivate students and build interest in the text or lesson.
- Provide the teacher with an opportunity to identify and correct misinformation about a topic prior to reading.

Types of Text

Concept maps can be used with both fiction and nonfiction text. They are especially useful for nonfiction text.

Steps

Preparation

1. Think about the content that will be presented in the text to be read. Identify an important concept from the text that students will need to understand in order to comprehend the text.
2. Complete a concept map for the identified concept. Develop a blank map for use with the students.
3. The simplest maps just contain information about the concept, almost in a brainstorming format. More complex maps show relationships among concepts and have many different levels. Be sure to choose the correct level of difficulty for your students.

Implementation

1. When you first introduce concept maps to your students, you should model the process of completing the map. You should complete the map for the students as they watch. As you complete it, think aloud through the process so the students can hear what you are thinking.

2. Gradually, as you complete more concept maps, have the students begin to take more responsibility for the completion. At first, have them help you, and then allow them to complete maps in pairs or small groups. Finally, when the students understand the process, they can complete concept maps independently.

3. Options for concept maps:

   a. Provide the topic and a blank concept map with a vocabulary word bank. The task is to sort the words into the proper places on the provided concept map. This is the easiest task, as the map and words are already identified for the students.

   b. Provide the topic and a blank concept map, but do not provide the words. The students must determine what words belong in the spaces on the map. This is more difficult than option a.

   c. Provide the topic and the words but no concept map. The students must identify the relationships among the words and develop the map themselves. This is more difficult than options a and b.

   d. The most difficult option is to provide the topic and ask the students to develop a concept map on their own. You do not provide the words or the blank map. This should only be used after students have had many experiences with completing concept maps in all the other options.

Counting Words

Counting words is an activity that supports the development of emergent literacy skills.

Purpose

The purposes of the counting words instructional strategy are to:

- Support the development of one-to-one correspondence so that students understand that there is one word spoken for each word in the text.
- Reinforce left-to-right progression through counting and modeling.

Steps

Preparation

1. Select several short sentences from a familiar story, or have the students dictate sentences.
2. Write each sentence on a sentence strip.

Implementation

1. Give each student a sentence strip and a handful of tokens, such as chips or beans.
2. Read the sentence aloud, and model for the students how you place one token beneath each word as it is read aloud.
3. After reading the sentence, count the number of words in the sentence. Then count the number of tokens. Show the students that the numbers are the same. Reinforce that there is one word said aloud for each word that is written.

DR-TA
Directed Reading-Thinking Activity

The Directed Reading-Thinking Activity (DR-TA) was first named by reading researcher Russell Stauffer in 1969.

Purpose

The purposes of the DR-TA instructional strategy are to:

- Support students' attempts to be active readers.
- Provide students with practice in monitoring comprehension.
- Develop students' skills in predicting/verifying while reading.

Types of Text

The DR-TA can be done with any text.

Steps

Preparation

1. Select the text for the DR-TA. Remember that the students will be making predictions, so select a text that lends itself to that goal.
2. Read through the entire text first, and select the points at which you will stop to ask the students to predict what will happen next or what a certain passage will be about. You might want to mark these using a small sticky note, on which you write the question prompt you will ask the students.

Implementation

1. The *D* in DR-TA means directed because the DR-TA is directed by the teacher. The teacher
   a. activates students' prior knowledge;
   b. has students read titles, headings, and other text features in nonfiction text to make predictions about what they think the text will be about; and
   c. asks the students to explain their thinking related to their predictions—*Why* is the student making that prediction? What text feature, vocabulary, event, and so on lead the student to make that prediction? You may want to write the predictions on the board or on chart paper.

2. The *R* in DR-TA means reading. The next step in the process is to have the students read to the first pre-selected stopping point in the text. Students should read silently whenever they are reading for comprehension. Tell the students where to stop, and ask them to put their finger in the book and close the book when they are finished, so that you will know when everyone is ready to continue.

3. When all the students are finished reading the section, the teacher asks whether their predictions were correct.

4. The *T* in DR-TA means thinking. The students should find support in the text and use it to demonstrate that the prediction was either correct or incorrect. Sharing the text support is a critical step that should not be overlooked!

5. The students then make new predictions, which are recorded by the teacher, and the process begins again. The same steps are repeated until the students reach the end of the text.

Dough Alphabet/Pretzel Alphabet

Purpose

Having students form letters from dough is a way to practice letter identification and letter formation while incorporating the tactile modality.

Steps

Preparation

1. Prepare the dough in advance, or allow the students to prepare it with you. Preparing the dough together is an excellent way to reinforce measurement skills and following directions.
2. Provide each student with a ball of dough and a placemat or piece of construction paper to use as a mat for rolling the dough.

Implementation

1. Show the students how to create a rope by rolling the clay on the mat with their palms.
2. Demonstrate how to form one of the letters of the alphabet by using the clay rope.
3. Practice each of the letters of the alphabet by having students create them as you call them out. You may want to place a letter card on the whiteboard as a model for the students to use or provide each student with a card showing each letter.

Extensions

1. Have the students create words with their dough. Start with their names, and then have them create sight words or other words they are learning.
2. Use the pretzel dough to create name pretzels. Bake them and eat them!

Recommended Recipes

Pretzel Dough Recipes

Super Easy Soft Pretzels for Kids
https://livingwellmom.com/recipe-soft-pretzels-for-kids/

How to Make Soft Pretzels Kids Will Love
https://www.highlights.com/parents/recipes/how-make-soft-pretzels

Easy No-Knead, No Rise Pretzels
https://anoregoncottage.com/easy-no-knead-no-rise-soft-pretzels-kid/

Craft Dough Recipes

53 Easy Homemade Playdough Recipes for Kids
https://www.kidactivities.net/play-dough-recipes/

Best Homemade Playdough Recipe
https://www.iheartnaptime.net/play-dough-recipe/

Echo Reading/Pointing

Purpose

Echo reading is an excellent activity for building students' phrasing and expression in oral reading. Books that have a lot of expressive dialogue work well for echo reading activities.

Adding pointing during echo reading is useful for students at the emergent literacy level. This can reinforce one-to-one correspondence, left-to-right progression, and concept of word. It is important that pointing is discontinued once students are beyond the emergent literacy stage. Continuing to point at words inhibits fluency development because it impairs the growth of the eye-voice span.

Steps

Preparation

1. Select a text that lends itself for echo reading.
2. Practice reading the text until you can read it fluently, with particular attention to phrasing and appropriate expression.

Implementation

1. Students should have already read the text silently prior to reading it as part of an echo reading activity.
2. You will read a short section of the text, providing the students with an exceptional model of fluent reading.
3. The students will try to echo what you have read—they should be encouraged to try to make their reading sound as much like yours as they can. Be sure the students are *reading, not just repeating* what you say from memory.
4. You may want to use exaggerated expression when reading to make the activity more enjoyable for the students.
5. Provide formative feedback to the individual or group who is echoing you. Tell them specifically what they did well when they read the text aloud, trying to sound like you did when you read it.

Environmental Print Walk

Environmental print is defined as print in the environment or surroundings. For example, signs, posters, billboards, magazines, newspapers, cereal boxes, and other food wrappers are all environmental print.

Purpose

The purpose of an environmental print walk is to help students begin to develop the alphabetic principle so that they understand that print has meaning. The activity can also help students begin to identify commonly seen words.

Implementation

1. Take students on a walk around the school or neighborhood.
2. Point out signs and other text. Stop to read them.
3. Discuss the letters the students see in the signs to help with beginning letter identification.
4. Use a digital camera to take photographs of the signs you see on the environmental print walk.
5. Use the photographs to create an environmental print book for the classroom library.

Extensions

As you take different environmental print walks, make new books or posters highlighting the print seen on each one.

You can also create some walks yourself to represent places that you cannot take the students in person, such as an environmental print walk to the grocery store, zoo, library, or other location.

Environmental Print Collage

An environmental print collage is a collection of signs, symbols, and logos that are found in the environment. Students create the collage by bringing in examples from home or finding them in magazines.

Purpose

Having students create environmental print collages:

- Focuses their attention on print around them.
- Motivates them to want to learn to read.
- Helps reinforce the idea that text has meaning.
- Encourages students to learn common words.

Steps

Preparation

1. Collect old magazines, newspapers, and advertising circulars to use for the collages.
2. You may want to ask parents for donations of these items.

Implementation

1. Explain to the students that print is all around them and that they need to begin to look carefully at print so that they can learn to read.
2. Provide the students with magazines and other sources of print. Have them cut out pictures of items they recognize and glue them into a collage.

Extensions

- Ask students to point out particular letters or words in their collages.
- Use the collages as inspiration for dictated stories or sentences.

Fact-Question-Response (FQR) Chart

Purpose

The purposes of the FQR instructional strategy are to:

- Support students' ability to generate questions about text.
- Assist students in identifying facts from expository text and responding to the information.
- Model for students the self-questioning process they should use when reading expository text.

Types of Text

The FQR instructional strategy is designed to be used with expository text.

Steps

Preparation

1. Prepare an anchor chart that will guide students in organizing the information, questions, and responses they generate from the text.
2. After the process has been modeled and is familiar to the students, they can work using individual FQR charts or can create their own charts in reading response notebooks.

Implementation

1. Students should read the text silently prior to working on the FQR activity.
2. If this is the first time they have done the FQR chart, model the process of completing the chart. Use a think aloud to model how you would identify interesting and important facts from the text to list in the *F* column, and then model how you would write question about the fact or a response to the fact in the *Q* and *R* column.
3. After the students are familiar with the FQR chart, they can work in pairs or independently to complete the chart. After the chart is completed, encourage the students to select one question they generated and to do research to identify the answer.

FQR Chart Framework

Based on the Magic Tree House series book, *Leonardo da Vinci*, by Mary Pope Osborne.

FACTS	QUESTIONS	RESPONSES
davinci was an inventor	What did he invent?	
davinci kept his ideas in notebooks that contained sketches of his inventions and his artwork		Wow! I keep a journal too! I am going to start making sketches in my own journals.
davinci painted the Mona Lisa	Who was she really?	

Fingerpainting Letters

Purpose

Fingerpainting letters is a tactile activity that is designed to be motivational and engaging for students as they practice writing letters.

Steps

Preparation

1. Gather needed materials: fingerpaint, paper, newspaper, paper towels.
2. Spread out newspaper on the students' desks or the table on which they will be working.
3. Give each student a piece of paper. Put a blob of fingerpaint in the center of the paper.

Implementation

1. Give the students a few minutes to paint whatever they want with the fingerpaints.
2. Tell the students that they are going to practice writing letters in the fingerpaint.
3. Call out a letter, and have the students write it in the paint. After you check their work, have them "erase" the letter. Call out another letter. Repeat this process for many letters, both capital and lowercase.
4. When the paint is beginning to get too dry, allow the students to make whatever they want on their papers and end the activity.

Fingerpaint Recipes

Paint Recipe for Kids: Homemade Fingerpaint
https://tinkerlab.com/paint-recipe-kids-homemade-finger-paint/

Finger Paint (Martha Stewart)
https://www.marthastewart.com/271805/finger-paints

Flannel Board Retelling

Purpose

The purposes for using a flannel board retelling are to:

- Support students' retelling of narrative text.
- Support students' recall of story elements.
- Motivate and engage students in the retelling activity.
- Provide an activity that appeals to the tactile modality.

Types of Text

Flannel board retellings are used with narrative text, as they focus on the retelling of a story and on the identification of story elements.

Steps

Preparation

Prepare flannel board pieces that can be used to retell a story. Inexpensive pieces can be made from tagboard. These can be colored with markers or colored pencils and then laminated for durability. Velcro tape can be attached to the back so that the pieces will stick to a flannel board. Felt pieces can also be made.

Implementation

1. After the students have read the story or have had the story read to them (for a listening activity), ask them to name the characters in the story. Produce each flannel board piece as it is mentioned. Prompt the students to name any characters they forgot.
2. Ask the students to name the setting of the story. Explain that the setting tells where and when. Produce any flannel board pieces that relate to the setting, such as a house or tree.
3. Have a student come up to the flannel to tell what happened first in the story, manipulating the flannel board pieces, as needed. Be sure you have modeled this for the students before expecting them to do it for you.
4. Continue with the retelling, adding each subsequent event and acting it out using the flannel board pieces.
5. Put the flannel board and pieces in a learning center, and encourage the students to retell the story to each other during center time or free time.

Suggestions

- Use a quick-stick magnetic felt board for the activity. These can be purchased online. They can be rolled up when not in use and will stick to any magnetic surface, such as a whiteboard or the side of a filing cabinet.
- Look for premade sets of flannel board pieces that can be used to retell popular stories such as *There Was an Old Woman Who Swallowed a Fly* and *The Mitten*.

Fluency Fast Phrases

Purpose

Fluency fast phrases is an instructional strategy that will support students' development of oral reading fluency. Specifically, it is designed to support the development of syntactically appropriate reading, smoothness, and reading rate.

Steps

Preparation

1. Write sentences from a familiar book that is on the student's reading level onto sentence strips.
2. Create phrase cards by writing commonly used phrases on index cards or segments of sentence strips.
3. Focus on phrases that include high-frequency sight words such as those listed on the Fry's Instant Word lists.

Implementation

1. Present the sentences to the students, and have them read the entire sentence from the strip
2. Hold up a phrase card, and have the students read the phrase.
3. Ask the students to match the phrase on the card to the same phrase on the sentence strip.
4. After reviewing five to ten sentences and phrases, mix them up. Lay the sentence strips on the table or the floor, and give the student the phrase cards.
5. Ask the student to match the phrase cards to the correct sentence strips by laying the cards on top of the correct phrases.
6. Students can be given the phrase cards to practice on their own.
7. Repeat the activity on a regular basis, changing a few of the sentences and phrases each time.
8. The sentences and strips should look something like this example from Rob Scotton's *Splat the Cat Dreams Big*:

His favorite books were about brave cats having daring adventures.

about brave cats

Alternative Activity

Create a shower curtain game that the students can use to practice the phrases independently.

Use a white or other solid-color shower curtain liner that can be purchased inexpensively. With a permanent marker, draw a hopscotch pattern or a path on the shower curtain liner.

Place one phrase in each of the sections of the path or hopscotch pattern.

To play, students must say each phrase as they hop, step, or jump into that section of the path. They can continue forward until they make an error. If they do, they must stop and go back to the beginning to start over.

© photographer/Shutterstock.com

© photographer/Shutterstock.com

Food Labels Alphabet

Purpose

The food labels alphabet activity is designed to:

- Support development of letter identification, especially the presentation of letters in a variety of fonts.
- Reinforce alphabet knowledge.
- Support development of sound/symbol correspondences.

Steps

Preparation

1. Collect a variety of food labels and boxes that present the letters of the alphabet in different fonts, sizes, and colors. Try to find one label for each letter of the alphabet.
2. Mount the labels and box fronts on tagboard, and laminate for durability.

Implementation

1. Introduce the activity to the students by holding up each of the label cards for the first five letters of the alphabet. Read the name on each label, and discuss with the students what kind of food would be inside that container.
2. Mix up the cards and ask the students to identify the label that comes first in the alphabet. After they have identified the *A* label, ask them to find the one that would come next, and so on. Arrange the labels in order on the whiteboard or on a table as the students identify them.
3. Put these labels in a learning center, and have the students practice putting them in order.
4. In a few days, repeat the process, introducing the next five letters. Repeat until all the labels/letters have been introduced.

Extensions

Use the cards as a word wall. Ask the students to bring in labels from home and hang these beneath the label card that begins with the same letter.

Green Means Go

Purpose

Green means go is designed to help students at the emergent literacy level with left-to-right progression and return sweep.

Steps

Preparation

1. Photocopy text that you will be using with the students for this activity. The text should be simple, predictable text with which they are familiar. You only need one or two pages of the text.
2. Using a ruler and green marker, make a vertical green line on the left side of the page. Use a red marker to make a vertical red line on the right side of the page.

Implementation

1. Ask the students if they know what a stoplight is. Discuss the use of green for "go," and red for "stop" on a stoplight.
2. Give each student a copy of the story to be read. Ask him or her to put a finger on the green line where he or she will start reading. Check to be sure that each student is pointing to the correct place on the page.
3. As you read the story aloud, ask the students to point to each word that you say, moving from left to right across the line.
4. When they reach the red line, remind them that this is a "stop" and explain that they must now go back to the start of the next line.
5. As the students become more familiar with the text, have them read along with you, pointing to each word as it is read and continuing from one line to the next.

Guess the Covered Word

Purpose

The purposes of the guess the covered word instructional strategy are to:

- Encourage students to take risks while reading.
- Model the process of using context clues, so that students learn to use semantic, syntactic, and grapho-phonic cueing systems when attempting to identify unknown words.
- Support students' identification of words they have heard orally but for which they do not recognize the printed word *or* words for which they have a concept developed but do not recognize the printed word.

Steps

Preparation

1. Select a short text passage that has a word that can be identified using context clues. Use a sticky note to cover the word that can be identified using context clues.
2. Use two sticky notes to cover the word—the bottom sticky note should cover all of the word except for the first letter, and the top sticky note should cover the entire word. Note: If the word begins with a digraph or blend, show the entire digraph or blend, not just the first letter—it is a chunk and should be treated as such.

Example

The boy and the girl ran down the street. They were carrying a bucket and shovel to use in the sandbox at the ▮▮▮▮▮▮	The boy and the girl ran down the street. They were carrying a bucket and shovel to use in the sandbox at the p▮▮▮▮▮▮

3. Remember to use the "inferring word meanings" activity before you use the "guess the covered word" activity with the students, as this will best prepare them for the activity.

Implementation

1. Read the page from the text to the students, preferably using a big book so that all the students can see the text at all times.
2. When you come to the covered word, just say, "Blank," and keep reading to the end of the page.
3. Go back to the sentence with the blank in it, and read it again.
4. Ask the students to think about what word could fit into the blank. Ask the students for suggestions. Write down all the suggestions on a chart or on the chalkboard. Ask each student to give you his or her reasoning for the word he or she suggested. This is the most important part of the activity. *Why* do they think the word they suggested might be correct? Praise their thinking, not just correct answers!
5. After the students have no additional suggestions for words that would fit in the blank, go back and read the sentence with each of the suggested words in place of the blank. Ask the students to give you "thumbs-up" if the word "sounds right" or "thumbs-down" if the word does not "sound right." For words that do not "sound right," discuss why they don't sound right and cross them off the list of possible words.
6. Carefully peel off the top sticky note so that only the first letter (or initial blend or digraph) is visible. Read the sentence again. When you get to the blank, make the correct beginning sound(s). Ask the students which of the words on the list can now be crossed off because they do not begin with the same sound as the covered word. Cross off all the words that cannot be correct. If the correct word is not on the list, have them think of new words that might fit into the sentence based on both the meaning and the sound(s) that are found at the beginning of the word.
7. When the students have guessed the correct word, uncover the word and read the entire sentence together. Remember to praise their thinking throughout the activity; the thinking process of using context clues and grapho-phonics to help them identify the word is what is important!

Highlighter Sweep

Purpose

The highlighter sweep activity is used to help students at the emergent literacy level to learn the return sweep needed when they move from the end of one line to the beginning of the next when reading. It also reinforces the development of left-to-right progression and concept of word.

Steps

Preparation

1. Write a short story on a piece of chart paper.
2. Create and duplicate individual copies of the story for each student, triple-spacing between the lines.

Implementation

1. Give each student a copy of the story and a highlighter.
2. Using a highlighter to point at each word, read the story aloud to the students. When you get to the end of the line, use the highlighter to make a "sweep" to the beginning of the next line. Exaggerate this motion as you model for the students.
3. Read the story again to the students, having them point at each word as you read it. When the end of the line is reached, they should make a sweep with their highlighters to the beginning of the next line.
4. You can use the same copies of the text several times by changing the color of the highlighter. Another alternative is to put the stories in plastic sleeves so that they can be cleaned and used again. Be sure to use erasable markers for the activity if you want to reuse the plastic sleeves.

Homographs and Accent/Stress (Supra-segmental Phonemes)

Purpose

This activity will help students learn that the accent they put on certain syllables in words is very important and that it can change the meaning of a word. This activity helps students with oral reading fluency and vocabulary development.

Steps

Preparation

Homographs are words that are spelled the same but are pronounced differently and which have different meanings. For multisyllable homographs, it is often the accent or stress placed on one of the syllables that changes the pronunciation and the meaning of the word.

1. Identify a set of multisyllabic homographs to use for the activity.
2. Write each word on a card. Use red marker to write the syllable that is stressed and black or blue marker to write the other syllable(s). Make one card for each meaning of the word. For example, if you were working with the word "produce," you'd have two cards that would look like this:

3. On sentence strips, write sentences using each meaning of the word.

Implementation

1. Show the students one set of sentence strips. Read each one aloud. Ask them if they notice anything about the target word.
2. When the students realize that it is spelled the same but pronounced differently and has a different meaning in each word, teach them the word "homograph." Use the word cards to show the students that it is the accent on one of the syllables that changes the word's pronunciation and meaning. Discuss the two meanings of the word.

3. Ask the students to read each sentence and sort the sentences according to the pronunciation/meaning of the target word.
4. Depending on the level of the students, you may want to introduce the idea that one of the homographs is a noun and the other is a verb. The stress changes the part of speech as well as the meaning and pronunciation.

Word List

Here is a list of words that work well for this activity. There are many others. After you teach these words to the students, ask them to find other homographs that change their pronunciation and meaning due to stress.

produce
import
subject
perfect
record
contract

Hula Hoop Retelling

Purpose

The purposes of the hula hoop instructional strategy are to:

- Provide students with a visual model while you are reading so that they can picture the beginning, middle, and end of a story.
- Support students' oral retellings of a story using a kinesthetic activity that has them move from place to place to signify the beginning, middle, and end of the story.
- Provide a model to support students' understanding of basic story structure.

Types of Text

The hula hoop instructional strategy is used only with narrative text.

Steps

Preparation

1. Purchase three different color hula hoops, or create three different color circles on the floor using yarn or colored paper.
2. Place the hula hoops on the floor in a horizontal line.

Implementation

1. As you are beginning to read a story to the students, step inside the first hula hoop. Be sure that if you are facing the class, you step into the hula hoop furthest to the right, so that, to the students who are facing you, it is on their left and you will be moving from left-to-right for them.
2. As you are reading, step inside the middle circle when you reach the middle of the story.
3. Continue reading, stepping into the last circle when you reach the end of the story.
4. Ask the students to verbalize what was happening in the story when you were standing in the beginning hoop, the middle hoop, and the ending hoop. You can have them physically move from hoop to hoop as they orally retell the story.

Extensions

To extend the activity, you can give the students a piece of paper with three circles on it, and have them draw (or write, depending upon their developmental level), what was happening in the story when you were standing in the corresponding hoop.

IBET (Text-Based Inferences)

The IBET strategy was first described by Linda Keating and Albert D. Lawton.

Purpose

The purpose of the IBET strategy is to give students a mnemonic device that will help them remember how to make text-based inferences.

Steps

Preparation

1. Identify a text that is appropriate for having the students make inferences.
2. Write some inference questions based on the text.
3. Prepare an anchor chart or reference card for the students to use while learning the mnemonic.

Implementation

1. Provide students with a copy of the text or display the text so all can read it.
2. Read the first text-based inference question. Model the IBET process for the students: Answer the question.
   I = Identify the inference that needs to be made to answer the question.
   B = Identify the background information the reader must use to answer the question.
   E/T = Identify the evidence in the text that the reader must use to answer the question.
3. Put the students in pairs. Ask an inference question about the text, and have each pair work on the answer.
4. As a group, review the mnemonic as you discuss the correct answer to the question.
5. Repeat the process until the students have internalized the IBET scaffold, and then allow them to work independently to answer some inference questions.

Illustrate Word Meanings

Purpose

The purposes of the illustrate word meanings instructional strategy are to:

- Encourage students to make connections between written and spoken vocabulary and images, to appeal to visual learners.
- Promote breadth of understanding of words with multiple meanings.
- Provide practice for students in selecting the correct definition for multiple-meaning words.

Types of Text

The illustrate word meanings instructional strategy uses lists of words that can be drawn from or inspired by any text. The words must have multiple meanings.

Steps

Preparation

1. Select a word that has multiple meanings, preferably from a text that students are currently reading or that they will be reading in the future.
2. Brainstorm a list of meanings for the word.
3. Prepare a list of sentences that use the word. Be sure each sentence uses a different meaning of the word.

Implementation

1. Post a word that has multiple meanings on a bulletin board, word wall, or chart.
2. Ask students to bring in a picture or item that shows one of the meanings of the word. If students bring in objects, use a digital camera to take a picture of the object or ask the student to also draw the item.
3. Students share their images and explain the word meaning that is shown by them.
4. After students have discussed the many meanings of the word, post the images on the chart or bulletin board. Put definitions of the word on cards, and have the students try to match the word meaning with the images. This can be used as a follow-up learning center to be completed individually after the lesson.

Extensions

1. You can also have the students write a sentence for each meaning of the word or match definitions to sentences you have collected and displayed for that word.

2. Create a "multiple-meaning words dictionary" for words that have multiple meanings. Use this to collect the words and images after the activity has been completed.

Insert/Vip/Think Notes

Purpose

The purposes of the INSERT or VIP or THINK NOTES instructional strategy are to:

- Provide opportunities for students to practice active reading.
- Support students' use of comprehension strategies during reading.

Types of Text

The INSERT instructional strategy is used with narrative text. The same procedure, when used with expository (informational) text is called the VIP (Very Important Point) strategy. "Think Notes" can be used with any type of text.

Steps

Preparation

1. Identify three to four symbols to use for the INSERT activities with the students. Putting these on an anchor chart will help students quickly learn the meaning of each symbol. You might also want to have the students generate the symbols.
2. Plan a think aloud to model the use of the sticky notes for the students. Show the students how you stop during reading to insert one of the sticky notes into the text.

Implementation

1. Explain the symbols used on the sticky notes.
2. Use your planned think aloud to model the use of sticky notes for the students. Show them how you use them during reading to indicate places in the text that relate to the symbol on the sticky note.
3. Provide each student with several sticky notes to use during reading. The number the students use will depend upon the length of the text that is being read. Don't give them too many sticky notes; students tend to use all the notes you have given them!
4. As the students silently read the text, they will use the notes to mark the place in the text that they want to share with the teacher and the rest of the reading group for the postreading discussion.
5. When the students are finished reading, ask them to share their sticky notes with a partner or with the entire group. You may want to share all of one type of sticky note

first—for example, all the sticky notes that indicate vocabulary words would be shared and discussed, and then those related to confusing areas of the text might be shared.

6. It is not necessary to share all the sticky notes after every reading; the important part is to get the students to think while they are reading; however, you do want to share some each time to encourage the students in completing the activity.

Suggested Sticky Notes

Use to mark interesting or unknown vocabulary

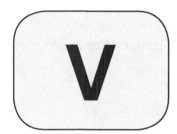

Use to mark parts that the reader enjoyed

Use to mark parts that surprised the reader

Use to mark parts that the reader is unsure about or that are puzzling

Use to mark parts that the reader used to make a prediction

Use to mark parts where the reader made a "mind movie"

© photographer/Shutterstock.com

Jackdaws

Using jackdaws as a reading activity was described by Timothy Rasinski in his 1983 article, "Using Jackdaws to Build Background and Interest in Reading," Eric document ED234351.

Purpose

Jackdaws are collections of artifacts that relate to a book. They are designed to capture students' interest and to motivate them to want to read the text.

Types of Text

Jackdaws can be used effectively with any type of text, nonfiction or fiction. It lends itself especially well to historical fiction, history texts, stories, and biographies.

Steps

Preparation

Collect a set of artifacts that relate to the text to be read. Suggestions for artifacts are photographs, maps, music, magazine or newspaper articles, books on related topics, biographies of the author, and realia, which are objects used in real life. For example, if you were reading a text set in the 1920s, you might include a flapper hat or necklace, a record of the ''Charleston,'' a video of people dancing the ''Charleston,'' a silent movie clip, newspaper articles about the stock market crash in 1929, photos of 1920 kitchens, and so on.

Implementation

1. Use the jackdaw collection to introduce the story to the students. Ask them to make predictions about what the book will be about based on the included items. Ask them to predict the time period or setting of the book.
2. The jackdaw items can be displayed in the classroom while the text is being read/studied so that the students can explore the items during their free time.
3. After students have been introduced to jackdaws, you can have them create a jackdaw for a book they have read. They can share them with their classmates as part of a book talk, or you might use them in lieu of a more formal report.
4. A similar activity would be to have the students create a "souvenir box" or a "travel trunk" for a character in the story. Students include items that represent the character's personality and activities in the book.

Jigsaw

Jigsaw reading is named after a jigsaw puzzle—each piece contributes toward the whole picture that is not seen until all the pieces come together. In a jigsaw reading activity, the text is divided into sections. Students are placed in groups and are assigned a section of the text. Students read their section of the text silently and discuss it with their small group.

When everyone understands their particular section of the text, the groups are mixed up so that there is one person from each of the small groups in a new group. In the new groups, each student then takes turns teaching his or her section of the text to the rest of the group. This makes the students accountable for reading and learning their section of the text. It also makes them responsible for listening and learning when their peers are teaching.

Phase 1: Small Groups for Reading
4 groups, 5 students in each group

Phase 2: New Groups for Sharing
5 groups, 4 students in each group

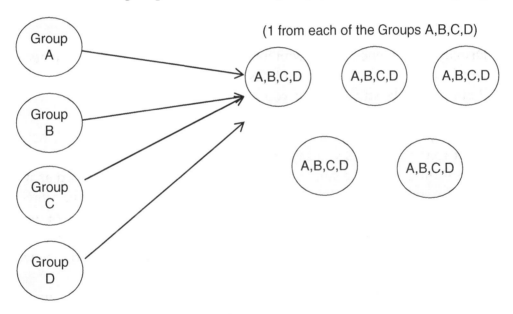

Teachers usually give a short quiz or assignment based on the entire text to ensure that all the students are individually accountable and pay attention when their peers are sharing. A graphic organizer or outline to be completed as the discussion ensues works very well as an activity with a jigsaw reading lesson. This approach is best used for nonfiction texts or textbooks.

Jumbled Sentences

Purpose

Jumbled sentences are used to help students at the emergent literacy level learn one-to-one correspondence, left-to-right directionality, and concept of word.

Steps

Preparation

1. Select a sentence from a text that is familiar to the students.
2. Write the sentence on a sentence strip. You will need two strips with the same sentence for each student.

Implementation

1. Display the sentence on the whiteboard. Read it aloud to the students, pointing to each word as you say it. Ask the students to read it with you.
2. Point out to the students that you are saying one word aloud for every word that is in the sentence.
3. Give each student one sentence strip. Read the sentence aloud, having the students point to the words as you say them, using their own copy of the sentence. Repeat this several times until the students seem to be pointing at each word as it is said aloud.
4. Give the students each a pair of scissors. Read the first word in the sentence. Demonstrate to the students that you are going to cut just one word off the front of the sentence. Cut off the first word that you read. Ask the students to cut off that word. Then have them cut the sentences apart, so that they end up with a set of word cards, with one word on each one.
5. Have the students "tornado" (mix up) their word cards.
6. Give each one an uncut sentence strip that contains the same sentence. Demonstrate how they can match their individual words to the words on the strip. Have them reassemble the sentence, using the sentence strip as a guide.
7. Read the sentence again together.
8. Send the sentence and word cards home for practice or place them in a learning center for the students to practice reassembling the sentence during free time.

Bobby and Skip ran down the road.

Bobby		

K-W-L
What I *Know*, What I *Want* to Know, What I *Learned*

The K-W-L is an instructional technique that was developed by Donald Ogle in about 1986 (Ogle, 1986a, 1986b). It is widely used in many reading programs and textbook series in science and social studies.

Purpose

The purposes of the K-W-L are to:

- Activate and assess students' prior knowledge about the topic(s) of a book that you are going to read or a lesson you are going to teach.
- Motivate students and build interest in the book or topic.
- Set a purpose for reading the book or participating in the lesson.
- Support students' active reading—asking and answering their own questions about text.

Types of Text

The K-W-L can be used with both nonfiction and fiction. It works particularly well with nonfiction text.

Steps

Preparation

Model for the students how you would complete the K-W-L chart. Use a think aloud to demonstrate how they will complete the chart. This is a critical step in teaching the students to use the K-W-L on their own and it should not be skipped.

Implementation

1. Guide the students individually or in small groups to support them as they complete the chart for the first time. Talk through the process with them, and complete the chart as a group, with each individual student suggesting what might be written on the chart.
2. After the students have completed several charts with your guidance and scaffolding, allow them to complete the chart independently when they read.

Variations of the K-W-L

Once students have learned the basic K-W-L framework, it can be modified to fit particular lessons/texts. Peggy Snowden identified a number of variations, including:

K-W-W   What do you *know*? What do you *w*ant to learn? Where can you find the information?

R-L-S   What did you *r*ead? What did you *l*earn? What will you *s*hare with the class about what you read?

T-L-I   Who gave the *t*alk? What did you *l*earn from the speaker? Why is the information *i*mportant to you?

References

Ogle, D. (1986a). K-W-L: A teaching model that develops active reading of expository text. *The Reading Teacher, 39*, 564–570.

Ogle, D. (1986b). K-W-L Group Instruction Strategy. In A. S. Palinscar, et al. (Eds), *Teaching reading as thinking*. Alexandria, VA: ASCD.

K-W-L Chart

K	W	L

Language Experience Approach (LEA)

The language experience approach, which is commonly abbreviated LEA, is an instructional strategy that had its origins in the early part of the twentieth century. It was popularized in the 1960s by reading researcher Roach Van Allen.

Purpose

The LEA is designed to support children at the emergent literacy stage. It helps students realize that speech can be written down and that they can read what they write. It helps students develop the alphabetic principle and builds knowledge of other emergent literacy concepts such as left-to-right directionality, concept of word, and alphabet knowledge.

Types of Text

The LEA uses a text that is dictated by one student or a group of students. The content of the text centers around a shared experience. This assures that the student(s) will have something to say.

Steps

1. Students should participate in a shared experience that will form the basis of the LEA. This could be a field trip, art activity, classroom visitor, holiday party, or even something as simple as popping popcorn in the classroom.
2. If students are dictating individual stories, regular paper can be used. Some teachers use paper that has lines at the bottom and a place for the student to draw an illustration at the top. If a group story is being written, chart paper is used so that all the students can see the writing.
3. Have the students dictate a story about the shared experience. Write exactly what the student says, regardless of whether it is grammatically correct or not. The student will be reading the story after it is written. If you change it, it will not match what the student says when he or she is reading it.
4. If you are working with a group of students, each student should dictate one sentence. You may want to include each student's name in their sentence, such as "Maria liked the smell of the popcorn."
5. When the dictation is finished, read the story back to the student(s), pointing at each word as you read it.
6. Each student should get an individual copy of the story to take home to read.

Extensions

Post the chart of the LEA story in the classroom. Use it to practice letter or sight word identification. Read the story with the students, and have a student use a pointer or frame to identify a particular word or letter on the chart.

Collect individual LEA stories about the same event and use them to create a class book about the shared experience, such as "Miss Smith's Class Goes to the Zoo."

Literature Circles

Purpose

The purposes of the literature circle instructional strategy are to:

- Support students' attempts to be active readers.
- Provide students with opportunities to read text and discuss it with their peers.
- Require students to interact with text so that they notice text features, writing traits, vocabulary words, and so on, depending upon assigned roles.

Types of Text

Literature circles can be implemented with any texts. They are traditionally done with narrative text but can be used with expository text if the roles are modified.

Steps

Preparation

1. Teach the students the roles you have selected for the literature circles. If you are using role guide sheets, prepare those for each role. Roles you may use include: author's craft detective, discussion director, passage master, summarizer, and word researcher, among others.
2. Students may select their own books, or you may divide them into groups to read an assigned book. Prepare the reading schedule so that students know what pages they must read each day.
3. Plan the role schedule so that each student has a chance to complete each role.

Implementation

1. Students read the assigned pages in the text and complete their roles.
2. Students get together to discuss the text. Each of them takes turns leading the discussion as they share their role tasks with the rest of the group.
3. After students have completed the entire text, be sure to assign a reading response activity.

Literature Circle Roles

Summarizer

- Identify important events, characters, and other elements of the book.
- Write a summary of the assigned text section, and share it with the group.
- Lead the rest of the group in discussing your summary. Revise your summary, as needed, to include other events or characters that your group thinks should be included.

Word Researcher (Etymologist)

- Choose three to five words from the reading. They might be words that you don't know, words that you are curious about, or words that you think are important for everyone to know.
- Write down the sentence in which you found each word and the page number (or line number) for that sentence.
- Prepare a vocabulary list for the members of your group. Include the sentences (with the target words underlined) and a definition for each target word.
  Your job will be to teach the words to your group members. Explain the words to the group and discuss them.
  Be sure to emphasize:
  - the origin of the word,
  - the meaning of the word in the passage, and
  - any roots/bases in the word that would be important to remember (e.g., "tele-" in telegraph means "distance").

Discussion Director

- Write three to five good discussion questions based on the reading. Be sure these are *not* questions that have yes or no answers, as those do not generate much discussion.
- Be sure your questions will get your group to really delve into the book and relate it to themselves, other books they have read, and to the world.
- Your job will be to keep the discussion going by asking your questions and prompting the other students as they discuss the book.

Passage Master

- Select two to three important passages or quotes from the reading. These might show important or interesting events, insights about characters thoughts/actions, foreshadowing, or they might be confusing areas that need to be discussed with the group.
- Your job will be to lead the group in discussing these passages and quotes.

Author's Craft Detective

- Read the passages as if you were a writer. Look for examples of the traits of good writing, such as ideas, organization, voice, word choice, sentence fluency, conventions, and presentation. (Read the information about traits of good writing, which we will discuss later on in the course.)
- Write down two or three examples of one or more traits. Include the passage from the reading, the page number, and what trait you think it is demonstrating.
- Your job will be to lead the group discussion of these traits. Explain:
  1. What trait is being demonstrated in the passages you selected?
  2. Why you think it is a good example of that trait?
  3. How the author's use of the trait improves the quality of the writing of the passage you selected?
- Ask the rest of the literature circle to add to your ideas and see what they think about the passages.

Media Master

- Identify two or three images, songs, or a short video clip that relate in some way to the assigned reading. Bring these with you to share with your literature circle group. Include the images with this role sheet when you submit it.
- Explain how the media you selected are related to the assigned reading.
- Think about the use of sound, color, and other features in the media you selected. How do they contribute to the meaning of the "texts"?

Little Book (Narrative)

Purpose

The purposes of the narrative little book instructional strategy are to:

- Support students' recall and retelling of text they have read.
- Provide students with practice in identifying story elements.
- Develop students' skills in associating visual images with ideas in text to build visual imagery skills.

Types of Text

The narrative little book instructional strategy can be used effectively with any story. The approach can be modified for use with informational (expository) text by changing the headings on the little book pages.

Steps

Preparation

1. Create enough little books for the students who will be participating in the lesson. If the students are able, you can teach them to make the books themselves. This also makes a great project for parent volunteers.
2. Prepare a sample little book that you have made for a former story that the students have already read.

Implementation

1. Show the students your little book, and either do a think aloud, demonstrating your choice of images and words for each page, or simply explain your reasoning for selecting the images and words to the students. This is a critical step, as it *models* for the students what they should think about when creating each page of their little books. Remember, the goal of the activity is not to make the little books, but to teach the students to judiciously select what they will include in the book and to identify appropriate visual images related to the text.
2. After the students have read the story silently, provide them with a blank little book to complete. You may have the titles for each page already written in the blank book, or you may provide a sample book that is blank except for the titles and have the students write in the titles on their own.

3. Following the completion of the little books, have the students share their books in small groups or in pairs. Listen as they explain what they included and be sure to have them explain *why* they chose to include what they included in their little books. They should also explain *how* the images they selected to draw represent the story.

Directions for Creating Little Books

1. Fold the paper in half, "Hamburger Style."

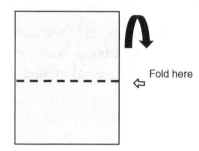

2. Fold the paper in half, and then in half again.

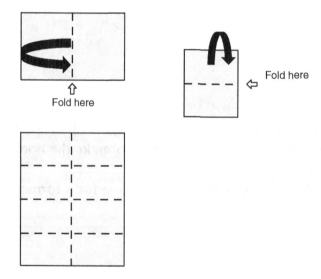

3. Open the paper up the whole way, and you should have eight boxes of the same size, as shown above.

4. Refold the paper it so that it looks like this:

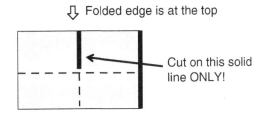

5. Cut *only* along the dark black line from the top fold to the middle of the paper.
6. Open the paper up and refold it "hot dog style" with the folded edge (and the small cut edge) along the top. It should look like the picture below.

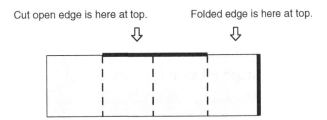

7. Pull apart the squares at the cut-open section of the book. It should look like this:

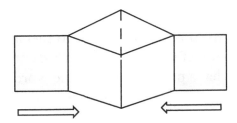

8. Hold at both ends and push toward the center, as if you were making a "fortune teller" like you made in elementary school!
9. When you have pushed the ends in to the center, you should be able to make the final folds in the book. You should have an 8-page book when you are finished!

10. Put the title on the front page. On the inside, label the pages: main characters, setting, initiating event, rising action, climax, resolution, my favorite part. For younger children, you can label the pages with the title, characters, setting, beginning, middle, end, and my favorite parts. Modify the labels depending upon the story you are using.

Logographic Word Cards

Purpose

The purposes of the logographic word cards instructional strategy are to:

- Encourage students to make connections between new words and known words
- Encourage students to use images to help them remember new words

Types of Text

The logographic word cards instructional strategy uses lists of words that can be drawn from or inspired by any text.

Steps

Preparation

1. Select vocabulary words for this activity that lend themselves to illustration.
2. The words should be from text that the students are currently reading or will be reading so that they will also have practice reading the words in context.
3. Prepare a sample logographic word card that the students can use as a model, using a known word.

Implementation

1. This works well as a long-term activity; students may have notebooks for the new words or word card files for their new vocabulary words, and they can add to them over the course of the school year.
2. The most difficult part of the activity for students is coming up with meaningful sentences. Be sure to model for students what a meaningful sentence is—and give examples of sentences that are meaningful or those which are not meaningful. A meaningful sentence must show that the writer knows what the word means. If other words could be substituted in the sentence for the target word, the sentence is not meaningful enough. In the examples below, the target word is ***dog***.
   For example, this sentence is **not** meaningful: *Bob has a <u>dog</u>.*
   It is not meaningful because many other words could be put in the blank. The sentence does not tell anything about the dog, so the reader can't tell whether or not the writer knows what the target word means.

By contrast, this sentence using the word dog is meaningful:

The dog barked loudly and then wagged its tail as his owner came home from work.

Notice that this sentence shows that the writer knows that a dog barks and wags its tail. It also shows that dogs have owners. There is a big difference between this sentence and the first, non-meaningful one.

In order to get your students to write meaningful sentences, you will need to model the process for them many times, using examples of non-meaningful and meaningful sentences to help them understand the difference. Try collecting examples of meaningful sentences from those written by your students; they will be proud to have their meaningful sentences shared. Come up with the non-meaningful sentences yourself.

3. Model the choice of pictures for the students. Explain to them why you chose the images you did for your example cards. Stress to the students that the images should remind them of the meanings of the words.

4. Logographic word cards also work very well as a computer-based activity. Students can create their cards using a provided template and can use word processing software to add clipart images. They can save their cards to a disk or a personal vocabulary file on the computer. To take the project one step further, you can have the students use presentation software, such as PowerPoint, to create a vocabulary quiz using their logographic word cards.

Sample Card Using a Root

Target Word	graph	Definition	to write
Meaningful Sentence The basketball star signed his auto**graph** on the ball.		**Image** © photographer/Shutterstock.com	

Making Words

Making words is an instructional activity in which students manipulate letter tiles or letter cards in order to make words. It was developed by Cunningham & Cunningham (1992).

Purpose

The purposes of the making words instructional strategy are to:

- build students' spelling skills
- build students' ability to manipulate sounds within words
- provide students with the understanding that they can look for little words they know and letter patterns in unknown words to help identify those words

Types of Text

The making words instructional strategy does not directly use connected text; however, to improve the activity, it can be done utilizing words from a text that the students are preparing to read. In this way, making words serves to teach spelling-based word identification as well as activating students' prior word knowledge before reading.

Steps

Preparation

1. Select a text that the students will be reading. From this text, identify one long word of at least six to eight letters. This will be the "mystery word" for the students.
   Example   Text: *Teach Us, Amelia Bedelia* by Peggy Parish
                    Mystery word: Bedelia
2. Identify 12 to 15 words that can be made using only the letters in the mystery word.
   Example   two-letter words: be, ad
                    three-letter words: bed, led, lid, lad
                    four-letter words: bead, lead, bled, lade
                    Mystery word: Bedelia (uses all the letters)

3. Plan the order in which you will have the students make the words. Begin with the smallest words and work up to the larger ones. Write down the cues you will give the students.

Example

a. Use two letters to make the word *be*. *I will be home after school. be*

b. Put those two letters back and use two different letters to make the word *ad*. *I saw an ad for cereal on television. ad*

c. Add one letter to the two letters you used to make ad, in order to make the word *lad*. *A lad is a small boy. lad*

d. Change just one letter in the word lad to make the word *lid*. *I put a lid on the jar so the tea would not spill out. lid.*

e. Change just one letter in the word lid to make the word led. *I led the dog down the street using his leash. led*

f. Keep all the letters you used to make led. Add one more letter to change *led* into *lead*. *The mayor will lead the parade. lead*

g. Change one letter in the word *lead to make the word bead. I lost a red bead from my necklace. bead*

h. Put all your letters back, and see if you can make the mystery word by using all the letters. Here is a hint: It is the last name of one of the characters in our book.

Implementation

1. Have the students get out the needed letter cards before you begin.
2. Each student should have a set of letter cards with which to work.
3. Lead the students through the making words cues that you prepared in advance.
4. If they have trouble making the mystery word, you can give them another hint or show them a page from the book with the mystery word covered. This helps them use both context clues and word identification skills to identify the mystery word.

Suggestions

Letter Card Storage

One of the main problems with this approach is that students tend to lose their cards. You can have each student keep his or her letter cards in a 5 × 7 manila envelope, with a paper clip or binder clip holding them together. Collect the letter cards after each making words activity.

An alternative storage idea is to keep each set of letter cards in a 3 × 5 file box, using alphabetical dividers to separate each letter. This works very well because it is much faster for the students to pull out the letters they need for the making words activities and the letters are less likely to fall out of a box.

Letter Card Sturdiness and Manipulation

Many students have difficulty manipulating the cards if they are simply created using thin paper, such as duplicating paper. You should make the letters on tagboard so that they are sturdier and easier for the students to manipulate.

Thin tagboard can be put through most photocopying machines, so it is still easy to create the letters. Laminating the letters is another way to make them sturdier; however, it would be very time consuming and expensive; given that you can simply make a new set of letters quickly with the photocopier, it would be better to save your laminating budget for manipulatives that take a lot of time to create.

Selecting Words

When you are selecting the words for your activity, use the "Words in a Word" website listed below to get a complete list of possible words. I find that if I put the words on index cards, I can sort them into word families or by other patterns. This helps me focus on one or two patterns in order to develop a lesson that is very focused and supports the students' word learning. Keep all the word cards in an envelope with the mystery word written on the front so that you can reuse the cards later on for a different pattern!

Helpful Website

http://www.wordplays.com/

Use the "Words in a Word" feature of this website to help you find the little words in the mystery word you have chosen.

Making and Writing Words

Making and writing words is an instructional activity developed by Timothy Rasinski (1999) as an alternative to the making words activity using letter tiles that was developed by Cunningham and Cunningham. It combines making words and word sorts.

Purpose

The purposes of the making and writing words instructional strategy are to:

- Build students' spelling skills.
- Build students' ability to manipulate sounds within words.
- Provide students with the understanding that they can look for little words they know and letter patterns in unknown words to help identify those words.

Types of Text

The making and writing words instructional strategy does not directly use connected text; however, to improve the activity, it can be done utilizing words from a text that the students are preparing to read. In this way, making and writing words serves to teach spelling-based word identification as well as activating students' prior word knowledge before reading.

Steps

Preparation and Implementation

1. Select a text that the students will be reading. From this text, identify one long word of at least six to eight letters. This will be the "mystery word" for the students.
   Example   Text: *Vacation under the Volcano* (Osborne)
                  Mystery word: vacation
2. Identify 12 words that can be made using only the letters in the mystery word. Look for words that you can use to emphasize patterns and letter chunks, such as -an, -tion, -ate, and others.

3. Prepare a making and writing words activity sheet for the students to use for the activity. List the vowels and consonants that they will be able to use for making and writing the words. Notice in the example that you write each letter that is found in the mystery word—if it appears twice, it is written twice. Put the letters in alphabetical order in the list.
   Example   Vowels: a a i o   Consonants: c n t v

4. Plan the order in which you will have the students make the words. Begin with the smallest words, and work up to the larger ones. Write down the cues you will give the students.
   Example
   a. In box number 1, write a two-letter word that means the opposite of out. (Give time for the students to write the word *in*.) Good. Words that contain *in* belong to the *in* word family. Another word in the *in* word family would be *pin*. Do you hear the *in* in the word *pin*?
   b. In box number 2, I'd like you to write a three-letter word that belongs in the *in* word family. Here is another clue—the word is a kind of metal. (Wait for students to write the word *tin*.)
   c. In boxes number 3, 4, and 5, write three words that would belong to the *an* word family. Remember, you can only use the letters listed in the boxes. (Wait for the students to write *can*, *tan*, and *van*.)
   d. In boxes number 6 and 7, write words that would belong to the *ot* word family. (Wait for students to write *cot* and *not*.)
   e. Think about the word boat. In box 8, write the word that you would have if you took the *b* away from the beginning of the word *boat*. (Wait for students to write *oat*.)
   f. In box 9, write the contraction for the word cannot. It is pronounced *can't*. Remember to put the apostrophe in the correct place.
   g. In box 10, write a four-letter word that describes a type of money that includes pennies, nickels, dimes, and quarters. (Wait for students to write *coin*.)
   h. In box 11, write a four-letter word that means someone who thinks she is very beautiful. A person like that would be called what? Here is a hint—the word rhymes with rain. (Wait for students to write *vain*.)
   i. In box 12, write a six-letter word that means something is empty—for example, an empty house would be called this. Here is a hint—it has the word can't in it, but without the apostrophe. (Wait for students to write the word *vacant*.)
   j. In box 13, see if you can find the mystery word that uses each one of the letters in the boxes. Your word should be eight letters long. (Wait for the students to find the word *vacation*.) If they need a hint, tell them it is something that many people do in the summer, such as going to the beach.

5. Select three "transfer words" that you will ask the students to write in the T boxes at the bottom of the making and writing words activity sheet. These are words that require the students to use the word chunks they learned while making the words in the lesson. For example, you might ask the students to write the word *coil* in the T-1 box for the example lesson, because they learned that in *coin*, the *oi* makes the same sound it makes in *coil*. Ask the students to write the word, and then ask them what other words they wrote have the same chunk in them—try to help them see that they can use

what they know about writing some words to help them figure out how to write new words. In the example lesson, you might have them write the following words:

Example   T-1   *coil*   (based on the *oi* in *coin*)

              T-2   *panda*   (based on the *an* in the *an* word family words)

              T-3   *nation*   (based on the *tion* in *vacation*)

6. Have the students cut out each of the words on the activity sheet to make word cards. They will then sort the words into categories that you provide. Think of your categories in advance so that you are prepared for the lesson. For the example, the following categories could be used for sorting:

Example

Sort 1   Words that belong to the an family and words that don't

Sort 2   Words that have one syllable, two syllables, or three syllables

Sort 3   Words that contain digraphs and words that don't

Sort 4   Words that contain blends and words that don't

Sort 5   Words that end in "n" and words that don't

Sort 6   Words that have words within them and words that don't (such as *ant* in *vacant*)

Some sorts can also be vocabulary/meaning-based rather than sound/spelling-based.

Sort 7   Words that describe things and words that don't

Sort 8   Words that describe how a person might feel and words that don't describe feelings

Variations for the Word Sort

1. Have the students develop their own categories into which they can sort the words. After they sort, have them write labels to name each category.

2. Have students add at least one or two additional words that would fit into each category after they sort the words. They can glue the word cards onto another sheet of paper, according to the categories, write the names of the categories, and then write in the additional words they thought of for each category.

Adapted from: Rasinski, T. (1999). *Making and writing words*. Reading Online. Retrieved from: http://www .readingonline.org/articles/words/rasinski.html.

Making and Writing Words

Vowels	Consonants
#1	#2
#3	#4
#5	#6
#7	#8
#9	#10
#11	#12
Mystery word:	

Making Words Grow

Purpose

The purposes of the making words grow instructional strategy are to:

- Support students' attempts to read multisyllabic words with prefixes and suffixes
- Encourage students to use analogy when identifying unknown words (looking for chunks of words that they recognize)
- Build students' use of morphemic analysis/structural analysis to identify unknown words
- Support students' spelling development

Steps

Preparation

1. Identify target base words to be used for the activity in a text that students are currently reading or which they have finished reading.
2. Select one or two words to use each day for the making words grow activity. Create a list of all the words you can think of that can be made from the target base word(s). Use this website for help! http://www.morewords.com/contains/side/

Implementation

1. Model the activity for the students the first several times they do it. After they are familiar with the activity, students can complete it independently.
2. Provide the students with the base word, and show how they can make it "grow" by adding on prefixes, suffixes, and other morphemes to make new words.
3. You can set a target number of words for the students to build (e.g., five new words or ten new words), or you can have a contest to see who can think of the most new words that can be made with the target word.

Mega-Cloze

Purpose

The purposes of the mega-cloze instrcuctional strategy are to:

- Provide students with support in retelling the events in a story.
- Develop students' listening skills.

Types of Text

The mega-cloze can be completed using any narrative text.

Steps

Preparation

1. Select a text that has a simple and at least somewhat predictable plot. The text should be in the traditional narrative text pattern; it should *not* be a cumulative or circular text pattern. The text for the activity should be a story that the students have already read.
2. In the mega-cloze, you will be deleting entire sentences for the students to fill in as you re-read the text to them. To prepare for the mega-cloze, read through the text and select the sentences that you delete. Do not delete any sentences from the first page or two of the story. There should be at least one deleted sentence for each student participating in the activity. Use a sticky note or light pencil mark to indicate the points in the story at which you will stop reading.
3. Write the deleted sentences on slips of paper or index cards. Write the title of the story on the back of the card in case one is misplaced.

Implementation

1. After the students have already read the story silently, use the mega-cloze to help them remember the story events in order.
2. Give each participating student one of the deleted sentences on a slip of paper or index card.
3. Begin reading the story. When you come to the first deleted sentence, stop reading and wait for the student who has that deleted sentence to stand up and read his or her sentence for the class. If the student is correct, continue reading until you reach the next deleted sentence. If the student is incorrect, and that is not the correct sentence,

ask if any other students believe they have the next sentence. If the correct sentence is not identified, you may give the first word or two of the sentence to help the student identify it.

4. Continue reading the story until all the sentences have been read and you have reached the end.

5. Collect the sentence cards to use again in the future.

Monitoring Logs

Purpose

Monitoring logs are used to:

- Help students become more active readers.
- Encourage students to question the text.
- Build metacognition and self-monitoring skills.

Steps

Preparation

1. Create a monitoring log for each student. They should look like the provided sample.
2. Select a text that lends itself to several different reading strategies, such as using context clues, visualization, using graphic organizers, and so on.
3. Plan a think-aloud demonstration that you can use to teach the students how to use the monitoring log, using the identified text.
4. Create an anchor chart to display in the classroom that provides the students with a list of possible strategies they could use while reading.

Implementation

1. Demonstrate the use of the monitoring log for the students as you think aloud while reading the text. Show them how to mark their logs to keep track of the strategies they used while reading.
2. Have the students read a text, and try using the monitoring log while you are there to provide assistance. Once the students are used to using the monitoring logs, have them use the log each time they read silently.
3. At least once a week or so, meet with each student to review his or her log. Discuss the strategies that were used and whether or not they helped the student.
4. Make notes regarding strategies that you need to review with the students.
5. Add additional strategies to the anchor chart as the students learn them and encourage them to try the new strategies.

Name _____

What I read	Strategies I used	Did they help?

Morning Message

Purpose

The purposes of the morning message instructional strategy are to:

- Support the development of concepts about print, including directionality, one-to-one correspondence, oral language, punctuation, alphabetic principle, and identification of common sight words.
- Create authentic literacy opportunities for students to read interesting content that is directly related to them.
- Provide opportunities for students to participate in interactive reading and writing with the teacher and with classmates.

Types of Text

The morning message is conducted with text written by the teacher or interactively written with the students.

Steps

Preparation and Implementation

1. Teacher prepares a simple text relating to the students' school activities, and students contribute to the text as it is written interactively.

> Today is Friday, October 30, 2019
>
> We will have music class and gym class today.
>
> Our fall festival is this afternoon
>
> What will your costume be?
>
> Xavier will be a football player
>
> Allison will be a doctor
>
> We will have apples and popcorn as a snack.

2. The teacher may allow the students to write words that they know as the message is written as a group.

3. The message is read chorally, several times, so that the students are familiar with the content. The teacher uses a pointer or hand to point at each word as it is read, to reinforce directionality, return sweep, and one-to-one correspondence.

4. To emphasize sight words, the teacher can give students magic wands, frames, or other pointers, which they can use to point to or highlight the specific sight words in the message.

5. The teacher may also choose to write some of the sentences in advance, leaving out punctuation or capitalization, or leaving blanks for the students to fill in.

Technology Connections

A digital morning message can be created using an interactive whiteboard. Teachers may write the message by hand or may use a program such as Kid Pix to model keyboarding for the students. Labbo (2005) suggested that the message can be read aloud using the voice synthesizer in the computer or software.

The digital message should be made available to the students throughout the day; they can use the voice synthesizer option to listen to the message.

The completed message can also be printed for students to take home or can be posted to the class website or daily blog.

Reference

Labbo, L. D. (2005). From morning message to digital morning message: Moving from the tried and true to the new. *The Reading Teacher, 58*(8), 782–785.

Onsets/Rime Flip Books, Slides, and Wheels

Purpose

Onsets/rimes flip books, slides, and wheels are ways to support students word knowledge. They are especially useful with students in the full alphabetic stage of word identification, as they encourage students to look for chunks in words.

English language is very irregular. Each vowel can make many different sounds. Most "rules" for identifying vowel sounds, such as the "magic e," don't work much of the time or only work for particular patterns. Instead of teaching students rules, teach patterns such as onsets/rimes to help them quickly identify many words. The vowel in a rime is more consistent than a vowel in isolation, so it makes it much easier for students to predict what the sound of the vowel will be.

Implementation

Create the onset/rime flip books, slides, and wheels for the students to use with you in lessons or independently at learning centers. After you have taught the students how to manipulate onsets to make new words with the same rime, they are ready to use the materials individually.

To enhance the effectiveness of the activity, after students have practiced a particular rime pattern, read a text, poem, or nursery rhyme that repeats that pattern so that they can practice it in context. For example, after teaching the -air rime, have the students read Rob Scotton's Splat the Cat book, *Up in the Air at the Fair*.

Onset/Rime Flip Books

To make an onset/rime flip book, cut a piece of construction paper into a rectangle. Write the onset on the right side of the paper. Cut smaller pieces of paper to make the onsets. Write one onset on each piece of paper. Put them in one pile, and staple them to the left side of the construction paper rectangle. Use two staples on the left side of the paper, so that the student can turn the page to the next onset to read a new word.

Onset/Rime Wheels

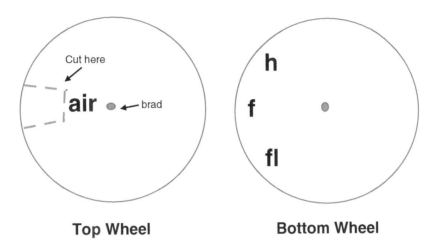

Top Wheel   **Bottom Wheel**

To create onset/rime wheels, cut out two circles of the same size. Cut out part of one circle, as shown. This is the area where the onsets will show through. Write the rime as shown on the example. On the second plate, write various onsets around the edge. You'll need to turn the wheel as you write them so that the letters will appear right-side-up when the wheel is turned. The easiest way to do this is to put the two circles together and then write the onsets as you turn the wheel. Use a metal brad to hold the two circles together so that the bottom circle can be turned.

Onset/Rime Slides

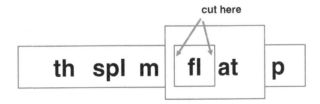

To make an onset/rime slide, use a 5 × 7 index card or piece of tagboard or construction paper. Cut two slits in the paper, as shown. Write the rime on the card.

Cut a long piece of construction paper or tagboard. It should be just slightly smaller in width as the openings you cut in the card. Write the onsets on the strip, leaving space between them.

To use the activity, slide the left end of the onset strip into the right slit on the card and through to the left slit. Pull it through, and the slide should move so that the onsets appear in a "window" in front of the rime.

Onsets/Rimes in Nursery Rhymes/ Poems

Teaching word families, or rimes, is a common approach for helping students learn to look at chunks of words instead of identifying words letter by letter.

Reading researchers have shown that words are identified faster in context than in isolation, so as much as possible, word identification activities should be situated in lessons in which students are reading actual stories in connected text rather than reading words individually from flash cards or on worksheets.

One of the most time-consuming aspects of teaching word families in this way is locating authentic texts that repeat certain word families. For young children, nursery rhymes and songs are familiar texts that can be used for this purpose. Texts can be created on charts or published versions can be used for word identification activities.

This list identifies many nursery rhymes and songs that can be used for common word families that students should be able to identify.

Nursery Rhyme	Pattern	Sample Words
A Bushel and a Peck	-eck	peck, neck, wreck
A Cat, A Mouse, and a Bumblebee	-ight	night, light
	-at	cat, bat
	-et	bet, yet
A Diller, A Dollar	-oon	noon, soon
All around the Mulberry Bush	-ice	nice, rice
Blow the Man Down	-eet	street, meet
	-ar	bar, spar
Donkey, Donkey Old and Gray	-ay	gray, bray
	-orn	horn, born
Five Busy Honey Bees	-un	sun, fun
	-eet	sweet, feet
Five Little Chickens	-ug	shrug, bug
	-eal	squeal, meal
	-atch	patch, scratch
Five Little Ducks	-ay	day, away
	-ack	quack, back
Five Little Pumpkins	-ate	gate, late
	-un	run, fun
Georgie Porgie	-ay	play, away

Nursery Rhyme	Pattern	Sample Words
Hey Diddle Diddle	-iddle	diddle, fiddle
	-oon	spoon, moon
Hickety, Pickety, My Black Hen	-en	hen, gentlemen
	-ay	day, lay
Hickory, Dickory, Dock	-ock	clock, dock
	-ive	five, hive
	-ine	nine, fine
Humpty Dumpty	-all	wall, fall
Hush a Bye Baby	-all	all, fall
If Wishes Were Horses	-ide	ride, side
I'm a Little Teapot	-out	out, spout, stout
Jack and Jill	-ill	Jill, hill
	-own	down, crown
Jack Be Nimble	-ick	quick, stick
Jack Sprat	-at	Sprat, fat
	-ean	lean, clean
Knick Knack Paddy Whack	-ee	three, knee
	-ive	five, hive
	-ine	nine, shine
	-en	ten, hen
Kookaburra	-ee, -e	be, tree, he
Little Bo Peep	-eep	peep, sheep
Little Boy Blue	-orn	horn, corn
	-eep	sheep, asleep
Little Tommy Tucker	-ife	wife, knife
Mary, Mary Quite Contrary	-ow	row, grow
	-ells	shells, bells
Miss Polly Had a Dolly	-ick	sick, quick
	-at	hat, tat
	-ill	pill, ill
Mockingbird	-ing	ring, sing
Monday's Child	-ace	grace, face
	-ay	day, gay
Old King Cole	-e, -ee	he, three
Old Mother Hubbard	-ead	bread, dead
	-at	cat, hat

(*continued*)

Nursery Rhyme	Pattern	Sample Words
	-ig	wig, jig
	-oat	coat, goat
One, Two, Buckle My Shoe	-en	ten, hen
Peter, Peter Pumpkin Eater	-ell	shell, well
Queen of Hearts	-ore	sore, more
Rain, Rain, Go Away	-ay	away, day
Rub-a-Dub-Dub	-ub	dub, tub

Nursery Rhyme	Pattern	Sample Words
Sally Go Round the Sun	-oon	moon, afternoon
See-Saw Marjorie Daw	-aw	Daw, saw, straw
Sing a Song of Sixpence	-ing	king, sing
Star Light, Star Bright	-ight	light, bright, night
There Was an Old Lady Who Swallowed a Fly	-at	cat, that
	-ow	cow, how
Three Blind Mice	-ife	wife, knife
Three Little Kittens	-itten	kitten, mitten
	-ear	dear, fear
To Market, To Market	-ig	pig, jig
	-og	hog, jog
Tom, Tom, the Piper's Son	-eat	eat, beat
Wee Willie Winkie	-own	town, nightgown
	-ock	lock, o'clock
What Are Little Girls Made Of?	-ice	spice, nice
	-ails	snails, tails
Yankee Doodle	-andy	dandy, handy

Related Nursery Rhyme and Song Books

Adams, P.	*There Was an Old Lady Who Swallowed a Fly*
Baker, K.	*Hickory, Dickory, Dock*
Bunting, E. and Fraser, M.A.	*Hey Diddle Diddle*
Cabrera, J.	*Old Mother Hubbard*
Caldecott, R.	*Sing a Song for Sixpence*
Church, C.J.	*Rain, Rain, Go Away*
Edwards, P. D.	*Miss Polly Has a Dolly*
Galdone, P.	*Three Little Kittens*
Galdone, P.	*Tom, Tom, the Piper's Son*
Galloway, F.	*Hickory, Dickory, Dock*
Hines, A.G.	*1, 2, Buckle My Shoe*
Kellogg, S.	*Yankee Doodle*
Kubler, A.	*Humpty Dumpty*
Loesser, F.	*I Love You! A Bushel and a Peck*
Raffi	*Five Little Ducks*
Reasoner, C. and LeRay, M.	*Hey, Diddle, Diddle*
Lewis, A.	*Five Little Ducks*
Miranda, A.	*To Market, To Market*
Salem, L. and Stewart, J.	*Little Bo Peep*
Salem, L. and Stewart, J.	*Mary, Mary Quite Contrary*
Taback, S.	*There Was an Old Lady Who Swallowed a Fly*
Trapani, I.	*I'm a Little Teapot*
Yoon, S.	*Humpty Dumpty*
Zelinsky, P.O.	*Knick Knack Paddywhack*

Partner Reading

Students enjoy working with their peers. Partner reading provides motivation for them to complete repeated readings because they are reading with a peer. Partner reading activities are excellent for building expression, smoothness (phrasing), and expression. It is especially effective if combined with peer assessment, feedback, and goal-setting.

Steps

Preparation

1. Create pairs of students who are on similar reading levels. No matter how you try, one partner will always be a slightly better reader than the other. Because of this, I like to give students two partners—one *even partner* and one *odd partner*. They pair with *even partners* on even-numbered days and *odd partners* on odd-numbered days. This way they have a chance to be the stronger reader in one pair and the less-able reader in the other pair.
2. Take the time to teach the students how to read quietly to each other without disturbing the rest of the class. You may want to teach them *shoulder-to-shoulder* reading for this purpose.
3. If you are using peer assessment and goal-setting, this should be modeled numerous times before students are expected to assess and set goals on their own.

Implementation

1. Set aside time for partner reading each day. After students learn the expected behaviors, partner reading can be utilized as an independent activity that students can complete while you are working with one reading group.
2. If you are utilizing peer assessment and goal-setting, this should be done once each week, on the same day—every Friday, for example. This will give the students the opportunity to assess and set goals with both of their partners.

Phrase-Cued Text

Purpose

The purposes of the phrase-cued text instructional strategy are to:

- Build students' fluency through repeated readings.
- Promote and encourage reading with syntactically appropriate phrasing.

Types of Text

Phrase-cued text activities can be done with any text. All activities for developing reading fluency should be based on texts at the student's instructional or independent reading level. Ideally, the students should have already read the text silently, in its entirety, before it is used for fluency activities.

Steps

Preparation

1. Select a short passage from an appropriate text. The text should be about 100 to 250 words long. Write the text on a transparency or chart.
2. Read through it yourself several times so that you can read it aloud fluently, paying particular attention to syntactically correct phrasing. Put slash marks / to indicate appropriate phrasing in the text. Use bold or colored font to make the marks obvious to the reader.
3. Also prepare two individual copies of the text for each student—one with the slash marks and one without them. Have students practice reading the text in different ways each day for a week. For example, use echo reading on Monday, choral reading on Tuesday, and so on. Emphasize phrasing and expression. On Friday, have the students read the text without the slashes, and you should notice that they are reading it with appropriate phrasing.

Example Phrase-Cued Text

A boy and his dog, / Max, / ran down the street. / They did not know / that a huge surprise / was awaiting them at home!

Picture Walk/Text Walk

Purpose

The purposes of a picture walk are to:

- Activate and assess students' prior knowledge about the topic(s) of a book that you are going to read or a lesson you are going to teach.
- Motivate students and build interest in the book or topic.
- Demonstrate use of illustrations (picture clues) to support text comprehension.

Types of Text

The picture walk can be used with any type of text.

Steps

Preparation

1. Read through the book, looking at the illustrations.
2. Jot down one or two sentences for each picture. Your sentences should
   a. use appropriate vocabulary that students might encounter in the book,
   b. point out important features of the topic that are illustrated by the photos, and
   c. not give away any surprise endings!
3. Identify one or two illustrations that you could use to have the students make a prediction about the story or the information in the book.
4. Identify several pages on which you can base questions to the students. Use "W" questions (who, what, when, where, why) to get the students talking about the illustrations.

Implementation

1. Show the students the illustrations in the book, as if you were reading it.
2. As you turn each page, talk about the illustrations, using the sentences that you planned. Do not read the actual text in the book.
3. Ask students your planned "W" questions to try to get them to relate what they already know about the topic to the illustrations they see in the book and to have them make predictions about the text.

Sample Statements and "W" Questions

- Let's look at the front cover. I see a frog on the cover. The book is going to be about a frog.
- I see that the frog is wearing a baseball cap and blue jeans. Do you think this is going to be a story about a real frog or about a make-believe frog? What makes you think so?
- On this page, I see that there is a fly buzzing around the frog.
- The frog's tongue looks very long on this page. Do you think he's going to try to eat the fly? Do you think he will do it?

Predictogram

Purpose

The purposes of the predictogram activity are to

- Activate and assess students' prior knowledge about the topic(s) of a book that you are going to read.
- Motivate students and build interest in the book.
- Identify vocabulary that students know or may need to learn.
- Assist students in relating vocabulary to story elements (characters, plot, etc.).

Types of Text

The predictogram is designed to be used with fictional text.

Steps

Preparation

1. Identify 15 to 20 words that would be important for the students' understanding of the text. The selected vocabulary words should represent the story elements: characters, setting, problem, action, and solution.
2. List the words in alphabetical order.
3. Provide the students with a predictogram chart to use for word sorting.

Implementation

1. Introduce the book to the students. Show them the cover, and read the title.
2. Ask the students to sort the words into the appropriate categories on the predictogram chart.
3. If you are using the predictogram as a way to assess students' prior knowledge of vocabulary in the text, collect the predictogram chart and analyze the students' work. This will assist you in selecting words to preteach or to highlight during book discussions.
4. If you are interested in activating students' prior knowledge before reading, review the predictogram after the students have completed it individually. Have each word written on an index card and use a pocket chart for sorting them into the predictogram categories or write them on sticky notes and sort them onto a reusable anchor chart. As each word is discussed, be sure to have the students explain their reasoning behind the choice of category for each word.

5. Students read the story.
6. Revisit the original predictions after the story has been read. Make changes as necessary. Move the "mystery words" to the correct place on the predictogram chart.

Follow-up Ideas

Word Wall

Use the word cards/sticky notes as the basis of a word wall to which you can add additional words as you read the text.

Writing Predictions

Have the students use the sticky notes/word cards to write a prediction about what the text might be about.

Predictogram Example

The Art Lesson by Tomie DePaola

Word Bank		
art teacher	artist	Chalk
copy	crayons	Draw
Fall River	first grade	Flashlight
Kindergarten	Nana	painting
pilgrims	sheets	Tomie
turkeys	walls	

Put each word from the word bank into the correct category.

If you are unsure about a word, put it in the "Mystery Words" list.

Characters	Setting	Mystery Words

Problem	Action	Solution

Question-Answer-Relationships (QARs)

Purpose

The purposes of the QARs instructional strategy are to:

- Support students' ability to answer questions about text by making explicit the relationship between the question and the answer.
- Assist students in generating and answering their own questions about text.

Types of Text

The QARs instructional strategy is designed to be used with expository text, but it could also be used with narrative text.

Steps

Preparation

1. Prepare an anchor chart that will remind students of the four types of question-answer relationships: right there, think and search, author and me, on my own.
2. Read the text that the students will be reading. Write several questions of each type, based on the text.

Implementation

1. Students should read the text silently prior to working on the QARs activity.
2. Introduce the four types of QARs, using the anchor charts you have developed. Explain each type of question and how the answer to that question is found.
3. Give the students the list of text-based questions you developed for the activity. Complete the first several questions together, modeling for the students how you figured out the QAR and the answer. Use a think aloud, if needed, to show the students how they should approach the process.
4. Have the students complete several questions as guided practice, as you are there to assist them with any questions. Discuss each question, emphasizing the process used to identify the question-answer-relationship. Emphasis should be placed on the type of question, not the answer to the question, for these activities.

5. If the students are successful with the guided practice, have them complete the remaining questions independently or in pairs. Bring them back together when all are finished to discuss the answers.

6. Once the students are familiar with the QARs, you can have them write their own questions. Specify the type of question they should write, or have them write a question, identify the type, and provide the answer. They can trade their questions with a classmate.

Types of Question-Answer-Relationships

Question Type	Relationship to the Text
Right there!	The answer to the question can be found right in the text, usually word-for-word.
Think and Search	The answer to the question can be found in the text, but the reader will need to gather bits of information from different parts of the text to answer the question. They need to think and search the text to answer the question.
Author and Me	The answer to the question requires some information from the text, in addition to the prior knowledge of the reader.
On My Own	The answer to the question is not in the text. The reader must come up with the answer based on his or her prior knowledge and experiences.

Radio Reading

Purpose

Radio reading is designed to give students the feeling that they are performing for an audience—that they are announcers "on the radio." It is effective in promoting appropriate phrasing, stress and inflection (supra-segmental phonemes), and expression.

Steps

Preparation

1. Find an old microphone, empty cardboard tube, or karaoke machine.
2. Select a text appropriate for "announcing"—perhaps you will want to have a student read the weather or classroom news for the day, similar to the announcements on the school public address system.

Implementation

1. Select a student to be responsible for the announcements each day. You may want to make this one of your "helper" categories. Each student should get a turn.
2. Inform the student the day before (or more) that he or she will be the announcer the following day. Provide the script that will be read to the class.
3. The student should read through the announcement numerous times in class and for homework until it can be read fluently. Listen to the student's reading and provide formative feedback so that he or she can practice again prior to making the actual announcement.
4. On the scheduled day, give the student the microphone and let him or her make the announcement to the class. Be sure to applaud when he or she is finished!

Reading Bingo

Purpose

The purposes of the reading bingo instructional strategy are to:

- Motivate students to read independently.
- Encourage students to read genre that they might not typically select for themselves.
- Build students' reading stamina by encouraging independent reading.

Types of Text

The reading bingo instructional strategy can be modified to suit any grade level or type of text. The provided sample is one that encourages students to read a variety of different genre, including both fiction and nonfiction, as well as poetry and newspaper articles. Teachers can modify the requirements of each block on the bingo form to focus on particular authors, text types, or genre.

Steps

Preparation

1. Prepare a reading bingo form for the students in your class:
   a. decide on the types of text/genre you want to include.
   b. arrange the identified texts into particular rows on the bingo form so that the difficulty level of the horizontal, vertical, and diagonal rows is approximately equal.
2. Duplicate enough forms for each student in the class.

Implementation

1. Introduce reading bingo to the students by reviewing the bingo form. Make sure students understand that they are to complete one entire line (vertical, horizontal, or diagonal) on the form during the designated time frame, such as one marking period.
2. Provide students with directions for documenting the text(s) that they read. For example, will you have them do a written report for each one? Will they discuss each text with you individually?
3. While the students are working on reading bingo, provide classroom displays of texts that fit into each of the squares.

Variations

To differentiate the activity for your students, it is very easy to have students working with a variety of reading bingo cards at the same time. The cards can include different texts for students who are reading below or above grade level, or you might have a student reading a few chapters of a chapter book to meet the requirements of one square on the card instead of reading the entire book. Differentiation can also be incorporated through choice of reading response activities for each student.

Have the students use the same reading bingo card all year long but require them to complete a different line for each marking period. This encourages an even wider variety of texts.

If you are concerned that students will choose short or easy texts, you can require that all texts be approved by the teacher in advance.

Technology Connections

Blank bingo cards can be printed for free at these websites:

http://www.bingocardprinter.com/bingo_blank.php
http://freeology.com/fun/blank-bingo-cards-template/
http://www.apollostemplates.com/templates-bingo/

Reading Bingo!

Name:

Directions: Choose one row of the bingo card to complete. You must read each of the texts listed in that row. Your row can be horizontal, vertical, or diagonal. Write in the title of the text you read and the date you completed it in each box.

newspaper article	biography book	collection of short stories	how-to book	series book
science fiction book	poetry book	magazine article	science book	historical fiction book
any e-book	mystery book	FREE SPACE	joke or riddle book	technology book
history book	series book	any book by your favorite author	humorous story book	world records book
nonfiction book	folk or fairy tale book	book about a famous artist	sports book	fiction book

Readers' Theater

Readers' theater is an excellent activity to use when you want the students to read over the text numerous times over the course of several days. Because they will be performing the "play" for an audience, they have a purpose for practicing. Remember that this is not a dramatic production—it does not need elaborate costumes and props. Keep it simple! Some teachers use name cards to label characters or use hats or other very, very simple props to enhance the production, but these are entirely optional.

Remind students that they are not expected to memorize their lines—they are going to be reading them from the script. Readers' theater is especially good for building expression and appropriate stress (supra-segmental phonemes).

Steps

Preparation

1. Select a prepared readers' theater script from one of the many websites or books that are available or create your own from a text that is on an appropriate reading level for your students.
2. Duplicate one copy of the script for each role. Highlight the lines for each character so that students will each have a script that has their own lines highlighted. This helps alleviate interruptions to the flow of the performance.
3. The first time students are preparing a readers' theater production, you may want to show them a short video of one from youtube.com or other websites. This will help them develop appropriate and realistic expectations.

Implementation

1. Students receive copies of the complete script, with their parts highlighted. Be sure to consider the reader's abilities when assigning parts. Some parts will be longer and have more difficult vocabulary than others; assign these accordingly.
2. Students should all read the entire script silently. After they are all finished, have the entire "cast" get together and read through the parts as if they are performing the play. This gives you the opportunity to make notes about individual student performance, so you can provide assistance to individual students if they are struggling with vocabulary, stress, or expression.
3. Over the next several days, students should spend time each day reading the script, practicing their lines. You may have them work in pairs—they should read silently the parts that are not theirs and read their own parts aloud.

4. As students are practicing, listen to each one reading his or her assigned part and provide formative feedback and support, as needed. Students should also take home copies of their parts to practice for homework.

5. After several days of practice, perform the readers' theater for the rest of the class or for a class of younger students.

Repeated Reading for Performance

One approach for building fluency is to have students do repeated reading. Practicing oral reading repeatedly, while effective, can be quite tedious and boring for the students. One way to motivate the students to practice reading is to give them text to read for performance.

Student performances can be held in "Poetry Cafes" or "Joke Fests" either for your class, other classes, or even for parents!

Suggested texts for performances include poetry, speeches, dialogues, scripts, monologues, and jokes or riddles.

Suggested Resources

Andrews, B.	*Poetry for Young People: Langston Hughes*
Dahl, R.	*Revolting Rhymes*
Giovanni, N.	*Hip Hop Speaks to Children: A Collection of Poetry with a Beat*
Lansky, B.	*A Bad Case of the Giggles: Poems That Will Make You Giggle*
Lansky, B.	*Kids Pick the Funniest Poems*
Lansky, B.	*My Dog Ate My Homework*
Lansky, B.	*No More Homework! No More Tests! Kids Favorite FunnySchool Poems*
Lansky, B.	*Rolling in the Aisles: A Collection of Laugh-Out-Loud Poems*
Lansky, B.	*What I Did on My Summer Vacation: Kids Funny Summer Vacation Poems*
Nesbitt, K.	*Revenge of the Lunch Ladies*
Prelutsky, J.	*The Dragons are Singing Tonight*
Prelutsky, J.	*It's Raining Pigs and Noodles*
Prelutsky, J.	*The New Kid on the Block*
Prelutsky, J.	*A Pizza the Size of the Sun*
Prelutsky, J.	*The Random House Book of Poetry for Children*
Seuss, Dr.	*There's a Wocket in My Pocket*
Silverstein, S.	*Don't Bump the Glump!*
Silverstein, S.	*A Light in the Attic*
Silverstein, S.	*Everything on It*
Silverstein, S.	*Falling Up*
Silverstein, S.	*A Giraffe and a Half*
Silverstein, S.	*Runny Babbit: A Billy Sook*
Silverstein, S.	*Where the Sidewalk Ends*

Rhythm Instrument Retelling

Purpose

The purposes of the rhythm instrument retelling instructional strategy are to:

- Develop students' memory of a story by using varied modalities.
- Encourage students to "step into a character's shoes" to see things from the character's perspective.
- Think carefully about sounds and relate sounds to the personality, emotions, and actions of characters in the text.

Types of Text

Texts with a number of distinct characters with a variety of personalities make the best choices for this instructional strategy. There should ideally be as many characters in the story as students who will be participating so that each student is actively engaged in the activity. An example of a text that works well for this strategy is *The Foolish Tortoise* by Robert Buckley, which tells the tale of a tortoise who removes his shell because he wants to go faster. Throughout the story, he meets a variety of animals who move in distinct ways, such as a horse racing by and a fish jumping.

Steps

Preparation

1. Select the book that the students will be reading and acting out.
2. Write the name of each character on an index card.
3. Gather a variety of rhythm instruments that students can use to portray the movements and personality of each of the characters in the story. These could include rhythm sticks, sleigh bells, cow bells, maracas, tambourines, and so on.

Implementation

1. Prior to this lesson, have students spend time using rhythm instruments so that they are familiar with them and the sounds they can make. Ask students to make their instruments sound "angry," "sad," or "excited." Help the students to relate tempo, rhythm, and volume to emotions.

2. Read the selected text aloud to the students or have them read it on their own or chorally.

3. Each student selects one of the index cards and becomes that character for the retelling of the story.

4. Students should think about their character's actions and personality in the story and select a rhythm instrument that they think best portrays their character. Ask each student to explain their selections; what was it about their character that made them choose the instrument they did?

5. Read the story again, as the students use their rhythm instruments to portray the actions that are occurring as the story is read.

Technology Connections

Record the retelling of the story so that students can listen to it later on. Use it as part of a podcast, or simply include it as part of the classroom's listening library.

Say It Like the Character

Purpose

The purposes of the say it like the character instructional strategies are to:

- Build students' fluency.
- Encourage students to read at an appropriate rate.
- Promote and encourage reading with expression, smoothness, and syntactically appropriate phrasing.
- Build readers' ability to empathize with the characters in text (put themselves in someone else's shoes).
- Recognize that authors provide clues to the feelings of the characters through word choice and punctuation.

Types of Text

Say it like the character can be done with any text. All activities for developing reading fluency should be based on texts at the student's instructional or independent reading level.

Say It Like the Character Variations

A variety of activities can be used for the say it like the character strategy. All of them build students' fluency.

Say It Like the Character: Using Word Choice and Text Signals

Authors use specific descriptive words and punctuation to help portray the emotions and speech qualities of the characters. Students should learn to look for these words and text signals to help them understand how the character is feeling and how the text should be read aloud (intonation, stress, volume, expression).

Steps

Preparation

1. Select text that provides examples of text signals and/or word choice that will provide clues to the reader who is trying to "say it like the character." You may want to start a collection of these text samples to use for instructional purposes.
2. Write the text samples on sentence strips, charts, or transparencies, so they can be seen by all the students in the group, and you can write on the text samples.

Implementation

1. The students should have already read the text for enjoyment prior to using it for the say it like the character activities.
2. Read one of the text examples while the students listen. Ask them to describe what you did when you saw particular punctuation marks or how you said certain words. Talk about how the author puts signals in the text to help the reader know how the character is feeling and would have said the text. Point out the text signals and word choices that give clues to the reader. You may want to underline them on the text samples or write over them with a highlighter to make them stand out.
3. Ask the students to read the highlighted text sample with you.
4. Repeat the process again, asking a student to read one of the text samples.

Say It Like the Character: Punctuation Detectives

Punctuation detectives is a say it like the character activity that focuses students on text signals.

Steps

Preparation

1. Select a text sample from a book that students have already read, and remove the punctuation from it.
2. Write the text sample on a transparency or sentence strip. If you use a sentence strip, make punctuation cards that can be inserted in front of the sentence in the pocket chart. If you use a transparency, the punctuation can be added using an erasable marker.
3. Alternatively, you can create several sentence strips of the same sentence or text sample, all without the punctuation. Students will write directly on each one with a marker.

Implementation

1. Ask the students to read the sentences silently. They should be told to think about how they think the character speaking was feeling and, as a result, how the character would have said the words aloud.

2. Point out to them that the punctuation is missing. Ask a student to add the missing punctuation, using an erasable marker (for a transparency), punctuation cards (if you are using one text sample and a pocket chart), or with markers, if you are using multiple copies of the same text sample.

3. After inserting the punctuation, ask the student to read the sentence as it would sound if the character read it that way. This is a chance to emphasize how commas, ellipses, question marks, and exclamation marks impact meaning and phrasing.

4. Ask if any of the students can think of another way to punctuate the text. Repeat the process. Keep repeating it until all probable versions have been tried.

5. Ask the students to think about how the character was feeling when saying the text, and try to help them select the version of text that would most closely match that feeling.

Say It Like the Character: Card Games

The say it like the character card games provide students with opportunities to practice the impact of emotions on phrasing, stress, accent, and intonation.

Steps

Preparation

1. Select quotations from children's literature (or write your own sentences) on index cards. The quotations should be from dialogue segments of the text.
   Example: "I wish you hadn't done that!"

2. Write emotion words on a set of index cards (e.g., happy, excited, upset, angry, sleepy, surprised, tired, puzzled).
   Note: The two sets of cards should be easily distinguished (different colors, different sizes, or some other distinction).

Implementation

1. Divide the class into groups of four to five students. Give each group a set of quotation cards and a set of emotion cards.

2. Select one of the following game-playing options:

   Version 1: Cards are placed face-down in two piles on the table in front of the students. One quotation is turned face-up so that it is visible to every student in the group. Each student then draws an emotion card, which they do not show to the others in the group. The students then take turns reading the quotation using the emotion that is on their card. The others in the group try to identify the emotion that is being portrayed by each student. When an emotion is guessed or each person in the group has guessed, play continues by having the next student repeat the process.

Version 2: Cards are placed in two piles, face-down on the table in front of the students. Students take turns drawing one emotion card and one quotation card. The quotation card is turned face-up on the table so that everyone in the group can see the quotation. Each student reads the quotation using the emotion indicated on the drawn card. The other students try to guess the emotion that is being portrayed. When every student has read the quotation, a new quotation is selected. Students return the emotion cards to the bottom of the pile and select new ones and the process repeats.

Version 3: Cards are placed face-down in two piles on the table. One quotation card and one emotion card are turned face-up so that everyone in the group can see them. Students take turns reading the quotation using the emotion indicated on the card. When all students have had a turn, a new quotation card and new emotion card are used and the process is repeated.

Selective Deletion Cloze

Purpose

The purposes of the selective deletion cloze, also called the modified cloze, instructional strategy are to:

- Teach students how to use context clues.
- Provide practice for students in using context clues (semantic and syntactic cueing systems).

Types of Text

The modified cloze instructional strategy can be used with either fiction or nonfiction text. The selected text should provide opportunities for students to use context clues.

Steps

Preparation

1. Select a text passage for the activity. The activity should provide opportunities for students to use context clues to identify words. The length of the passage should be 25 to 50 words for students in grades 2 to 3 or 50to 100 words for students in grade 4.
2. Read through the passage for the purpose of identifying words that could be identified using only context clues. Select no more than one word per paragraph, and do not select words that are in the first or last paragraph of the text.
3. Delete the words from the text. You may retype the text and put in a blank line in place of each deleted word, or you can photocopy the text, blank out the words using whiteout or white correction tape, and then make photocopies of the text for use with the students.

Implementation

1. When first teaching students how to complete a modified cloze activity, use a transparency of the text or rewrite the text on chart paper so that you can demonstrate and model for the students how they should think about the text and use the context clues to determine the missing word.

2. Always discuss the students' choices so that you can hear their reasoning for selecting the words they put in each blank. This helps you determine whether or not they are using context clues or if they are trying to use other clues, such as the length of the blank.

3. After students are familiar with the activity, they can complete the activity independently, but you should try to review it together so that all of the students benefit from the thinking of their peers.

Semantic Impressions/Story Impressions

Semantic impressions/story impressions is a teaching strategy that is used before reading a text. It involves having students utilize vocabulary from the text to make predictions about what they will be reading.

Purpose

The purposes of story impressions/semantic impressions are to:

- Activate and assess students' prior knowledge about the topic(s) of a text that you are going to be reading.
- Motivate students and build interest in the text.
- Set a purpose for reading the text.
- Model the process of making reasonable predictions about text based on vocabulary to encourage students' active reading.

Types of Text

Semantic impressions is a strategy that can be used with nonfiction text. When it is used with fictional text, it is called story impressions.

Steps

Preparation

1. Select vocabulary words from the text that will be read by the students. List the words in the order that they appear in the text.
2. Put the words on a chart or transparency so they can be seen by the entire class. Alternatively, you can list the words individually on index cards so that they can be added to the word wall following the reading of the text.

Implementation

1. Show the students the cover of the book, and ask them to point out details that they see on the cover that might be clues to what the book will be about. As they are making predictions, note to yourself whether they are using the vocabulary that they will encounter in the text and whether they seem to have a good understanding of the

concepts that will be introduced in the text. This is an opportunity to assess their prior knowledge related to the topic.

2. Show the students the list of words, and read through the list to make sure the students can recognize each word. If they are unsure of a word, tell them what it is and spend some time building the concept behind the word so that they understand it. When you are sure the students understand the words, move to the next step.

3. Tell the students that they are going to be writing a story (fiction) or article (nonfiction) using all the words on the list. Words must be used in the order in which they appear on the list, but endings may be added. For example, if the word "capture" is on the list, students may use the words "captured" or "capturing" in their stories/articles. Words may be used more than once. The students should be told that their task is to write what they predict might be in the book, based on the words. The first time you do a semantic or story impression activity, you should write the story or article as a group, so that the students have a model of the process. After they are familiar with the activity, they may write individual stories/articles.

4. After the story/article is completed, the students read the real story or text.

Follow-up Activity: Venn Diagram Comparison

Students may create a Venn diagram to compare the real story/article with the predicted version.

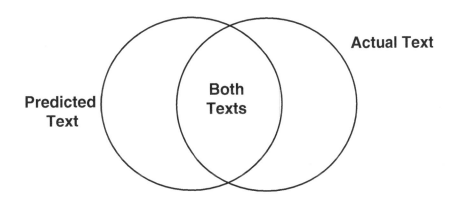

Sentence Starters (Text-Dependent Questions)

Purpose

The sentence starters instructional strategy is designed to help students write excellent responses to answer text-dependent questions.

Types of Text

Any kind of text can be used for this activity. It's best to vary the text type, as the sentence starters used for nonfiction may vary from those used for fiction.

Steps

Implementation

1. After students finish reading a text, pose a text-dependent question about the text.
2. Write down the students answers on a chart or whiteboard. Ask them to keep answering the same question, but to use a different beginning for the answer. For example:
   - Based on _____ on page _____, I think that _____.
   - Because this character said _____ on page _____, I think_____.
   - The chart on page _____ shows that _____.
   - According to the author, _____.
   - On page _____, it says that _____.
3. Use a highlighter to draw attention to the words used to start each sentence. Create an anchor chart showing these sentence starters to give students a reference to use when they are answering text-dependent questions.
4. As the students answer text-dependent questions, add any new formats that students use to the list of sentence starters.

Song Retelling

Song retelling is an instructional strategy in which students retell a story they have read by making the retelling into song lyrics and singing the retelling.

Purpose

The purposes of the song retelling instructional strategy are to:

- Encourage students to utilize music to help them retell a story.
- Motivate students to retell a story.
- Encourage students to think about word choice and sentence fluency as they convert the story into song lyrics.

Types of Text

Students can use any narrative text as the basis for a song retelling. A fun book to use to introduce this activity is *Click Clack Moo: Cows That Type* by Doreen Cronin. It is humorous, has a well-defined plot, and lends itself to a repeated refrain.

Steps

Preparation

1. Select a narrative text for the activity.
2. Read the text aloud to the students, or have them read it independently.

Implementation

Students should be directed to:

1. Think about a simple song that they know, such as "Twinkle, Twinkle, Little Star," "The Farmer in the Dell," "Row, Row, Row Your Boat," or other children's song that everyone in their group knows.
2. Jot down the important information about the story that should be included in the retelling. Be sure to have the main characters, the setting, and the main plot events included.
3. Work together to develop the story retelling to the tune of the children's song they selected. Be sure to retell the entire story.
4. When they finish writing the song, practice it quietly so they are ready to perform it for their classmates.

SQ3R/SQ4R

SQ3R and SQ4R are mnemonics to teach students to help them remember how to interact effectively with informational text. SQ3R is "Survey, Question, Read, Recite, Review," and SQ4R is "Survey, Question, Read, recite, Review, Reflect." SQ3R was first introduced in 1946 by educator Francis P. Robinson.

Purpose

SQ3R and SQ4R are designed to:

- Provide students with a framework to use to interact with text.
- Support students' learning from informational text.

Steps

Preparation

1. Prepare an anchor chart that can be used as a reminder of each step of the process.
2. Select a short chapter from a science or social studies textbook to use to teach the steps to the students.

Implementation

1. Model each step for the students using the identified text. After you model it for them, ask them to do it themselves.
2. Before moving to the next step, ask students if they have any questions.
3. When all the steps have been reviewed, have the students practice the process with a partner.
4. Each time you assign a chapter to be read in an informational textbook, remind the students to follow the SQ3R or SQ4R process.

SQ3R/SQ4R

S = **Survey**: Look through the text. Look at the photographs, charts, graphs, and other images. Read the boldface words. Think about what the chapter might be about.

Q = **Question**: Read the headings. Turn them into questions. For example, if the heading is "Plants of New Zealand," you might turn it into the question, "What types of plants are found in New Zealand?" This will help you pull out important information from that section of the text when you read it.

R = Read: Read the text.

R = Recite: Read the questions you created from the headings. Say the answers to the questions aloud.

R = Review: In your own words, summarize what you just read.

R = Reflect: Think about how the information you learned will be helpful to you in the future.

Story Glove

Purpose

The purposes of the story glove instructional strategy are to:

- Motivate students to participate in story retellings.
- Provide a framework to assist students in retelling a story by reminding them of the story elements.
- Assist students in remembering story elements.

Types of Text

The story glove instructional strategy can be done with any narrative text. It is an excellent activity to use to introduce the idea of summarizing a text or as practice in summarizing for a postreading activity.

Steps

Preparation

1. Prepare a story glove using a light-colored, fabric garden glove or a baseball glove. Write with a permanent, sharp-point, black marker:

thumb	characters
pointer finger	setting
middle finger	problem
ring finger	events
pinky	ending

2. You may also prepare paper gloves for students to use on their own, if you choose to do so. Use the pattern provided, and cut the gloves from construction paper or tagboard.

Implementation

1. Demonstrate to the students that they can use the gloves to remind themselves of what story elements need to be included in a retelling.
2. If you are using paper gloves for manipulatives, have the students label them with the story element names, following your glove as a pattern.

Story Interpretation

Purpose

The purposes of the story interpretation instructional strategy are to:

- Encourage students to pay close attention to the relationships between emotions in the story and the colors/shapes used in the illustrations.
- Provide opportunities for students to express themselves creatively through the arts.

Types of Text

Story interpretation can be completed using any text, particular texts that portray easily identified emotion.

Steps

Preparation

1. Students should have already completed preparatory activities that have familiarized them with the ways illustrators use color and shape to portray emotion in images.
2. Select the text that you will read to the students as a model text. Plan the think aloud you will use to model for the students how they should think about the text when selecting appropriate colors and images to portray the emotions in the story.
3. Create a sample story interpretation picture for the model text. Remember, you can only use shapes and colors—no recognizable objects—in your picture.

Implementation

1. Show the students some examples of visual art that do not include any recognizable objects—just shapes and colors—and ask them to tell you how the images make them feel. Relate the feelings to the colors and shapes used by the artists.
2. Read the model text to the students, without showing the pictures or illustrations.
3. Do your think aloud for the students, modeling how and why you selected the shapes and colors that you used in your story interpretation picture.
4. When you are confident that the students understand the process, explain to them that they will be creating pictures to go with a text that you will read to them. Their task will be to create a picture that portrays the story/text by only using colors and shapes. They may not use any recognizable objects.

5. Read the story for the activity to the students, without showing them the illustrations. Remind them that their pictures should capture the feelings portrayed in the text.

6. When the students have finished their story interpretation pictures, have them explain orally or in writing:

    a. Why they selected the colors they used in their pictures? How do the colors portray the feeling of the story?

    b. Why they selected the shapes they used in their pictures? How do the shapes portray the feeling of the story?

Story Map

A story map is a graphic display of the narrative story elements. They come in many different formats.

Purpose

A story map is designed to help students identify the narrative story elements. It helps students learn what information they need to pull out of a story when they are reading.

Types of Text

Since the story map focuses on narrative story elements, it must be used with narrative texts.

Steps

Preparation

1. Use a chart to create a large story map that can be used with a group of students.
2. Duplicate individual copies of the blank story map so that each child has his or her own copy.

Implementation

1. After students have finished reading a story, begin discussing each of the story elements. Explain what the setting is, and ask the students to name the setting of the story they just read. Write the information about the setting in the appropriate spot on the story map chart, and then have the students write it on their individual story maps.
2. Review each of the story elements in turn, filling in the chart story map and having the students complete their own maps.
3. After you have done this several times as a group with different stories, students can then be given story maps to complete on their own after reading narrative texts.

Narrative Text: Story Elements

Narrative text has certain elements that are consistently found in all texts. Learning about these *story elements* assists children in reading narrative text, because they build schema for stories and use these to make predictions when they read.

Story Elements

Setting

The setting is the *where* and *when* in a story. In some cases, the setting is explicitly identified by the author—for example, "It was a sunny day in February 1882 when Sophia stepped off the ship from Europe onto the New York soil." In many stories, the setting is less specific. For example, it may be possible to tell if the story is set in the present or in the past, but not exactly when it occurred, or it may be possible to tell if the story is set on an island or in the city, but not specifically which ones.

Characters

The characters are the *who* in the story. This is who the story is about. The actions in the story are carried out by the characters. Characters can be people, animals, or objects. The most important characters in a story are called *main characters*. The other characters are called *secondary characters*. The *protagonist* is the main "good character," and the *antagonist* is the main "bad character."

Plot

Plot is the *what* of a story. The events in the story make up the plot. It is possible to look at different parts of the plot:

- **Exposition**
  Exposition usually occurs at the beginning of a story to "set the stage," but it may also occur when new characters or scenes are introduced as the plot progresses. This can include events that happened before the story began (the *backstory*), details about the setting, and character descriptions. Exposition may also help to set the mood or explain the theme of the story.
- **Initiating Event**
  The initiating event is the starting action of the story. This is the beginning of the conflict and sets the entire plot in motion.
- **Rising Action**
  Rising actions are the events in the story that occur after the initiating event, but before the climax. These events help the story build toward the conclusion.
- **Climax**
  The climax is the high point of the story; this is when there is the most suspense or when the turning point is reached. The initiating event and rising action have been building and building suspense or excitement, and the peak of the building excitement is the climax.
- **Falling Action**
  The falling action occurs after the climax. In this part of the story, the author ties up all the loose ends and reveals how the problem was solved (if it is a mystery).
- **Resolution**
  The resolution is the ending of the story. The adventure is completed and has been explained.

Story Map

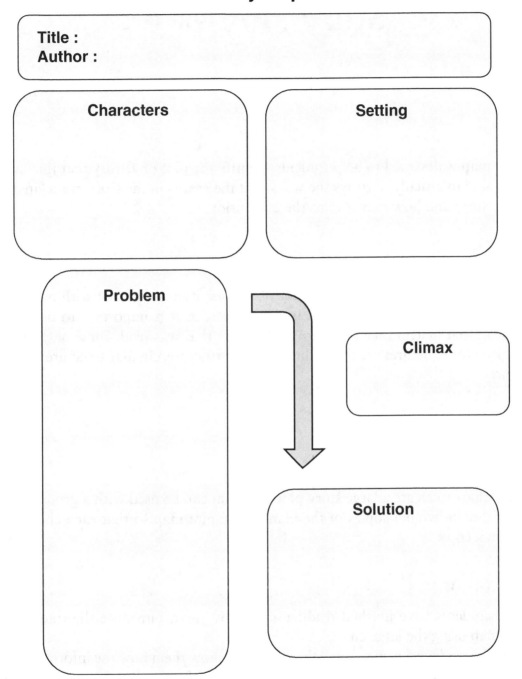

Title :
Author :

Characters

Setting

Problem

Climax

Solution

Story Plot Map

Purpose

A story plot map is designed to help students identify the plot of a story that they have read. The story plot map visually portrays the ways that the events in the story are related to other events in the story and how they lead to the conclusion.

Types of Text

Since the story plot map focuses on the plot of a story, it must be used with narrative texts. There are different story plot structures in narrative text. It is important to use the correct story plot map that matches the structure of the story that was read. Some of the most common narrative plot structures are the traditional plot structure, circular structure, and cumulative structure.

Steps

Preparation

1. Use a chart to create a large story plot map that can be used with a group of students.
2. Duplicate individual copies of the blank story plot map so that each child has his or her own copy.

Implementation

1. After students have finished reading a narrative text, introduce the traditional story plot map using the large chart.
2. Have the students begin to retell the story, and show them how the information fits into the plot map. Write the information in the correct place on the chart, and then have the students fill it in on their own story plot maps.
3. Once the students have become familiar with the traditional story plot map and have practiced it several times, introduce the other plot maps (circular, cumulative). Help them match the correct plot map to each story they read and practice using the maps following their reading.

Story Plot Map: Typical Narrative Text Structure

Typical narrative text can be displayed graphically using a story plot map. The plot in a narrative text generally follows a typical pattern:

* introduction of characters and setting
* a problem/initiating event or "complication"
*actions taken to try to solve the problem
*a climax or turning point
*the resolution to the problem.

The plot map for a typical narrative text looks like this:

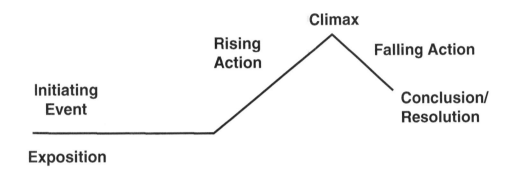

Story Plot Map: Cumulative Text

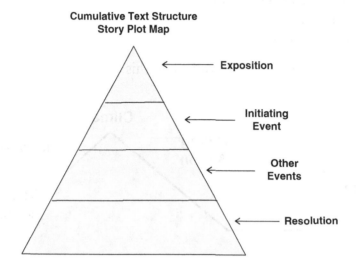

Cumulative Text Structure
Story Plot Map

- Exposition
- Initiating Event
- Other Events
- Resolution

Cumulative Text Structure

Cumulative stories begin with exposition and an initiating event. Rather than following the typical rising action/climax/falling action pattern of most narrative text, cumulative texts repeat events over, with the addition of new characters or items. For example, in the traditional story *Henny Penny*, Henny Penny is hit on the head with an acorn and thinks the sky is falling. She decides to go to tell the king. On her way, she meets numerous characters, including Ducky Lucky, Lucy Goosey, and Turkey Lurkey. As she meets each one, she tells him that the sky is falling. The new character joins in the trip to see the king, and the group moves on its way until the characters meet the next new character. This is basically the same scene repeated numerous times, which is what makes the story a "cumulative" story. Some stories go in reverse, as one less character or item is lost at each step. That graphic would be an inverted triangle.

Story Plot Map: Circular Text

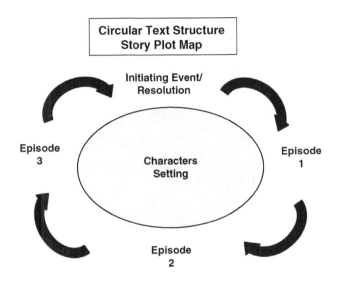

Circular Text Structure

Circular stories begin with exposition and an initiating event. The characters and setting are gradually introduced. There are numerous episodes that occur, but none of them move the action forward—they are not rising action, because they are not leading toward a climax. Several episodes occur, and the story ends in the same place in which it started. The resolution of the story is identical to or very similar to the initiating event.

Books with Cumulative and Circular Plot Structure

Cumulative Plot

Andrews-Goebel, N.	*The Pot that Juan Built*
Bishop, G.	*Chicken Licken*
Burningham, R.	*Mr. Gumpy's Outing*
Dragonwagon, C.	*This Is the Bread I Baked for Ned*
Duff, M.	*Rum, Pum, Pum*
Emberley, B.	*Drummer Hoff*
Fox, M.	*Shoes from Grandpa*
Galdone, P.	*The Gingerbread Man*
Galdone, P.	*Henny Penny*
Kalan, R.	*Jump, Frog, Jump!*
Kellogg, S.	*There Was an Old Woman*
Manushkin, F.	*Matzah That Papa Brought Home*
Oxenbury, H.	*The Great Big Enormous Turnip*
Stow, J.	*The House That Jack Built*
Stutson, C.	*By the Light of the Halloween Moon*
Taback, S.	*There Was an Old Lady Who Swallowed a Fly*
Taback, S.	*This Is the House That Jack Built*
Tolstoy, A.	*The Great Big Enormous Turnip*
Van Laan, N.	*Possum Come-A-Knockin'*
Williams, L.	*The Little Old Lady Who Was Not Afraid of Anything*
Wood, A.	*The Napping House*

Circular Plot

Aardema, V.	*Why Mosquitoes Buzz in People's Ears*
Agee, J.	*Terrific*
Arnosky, J.	*Every Autumn Comes the Bear*
Baker, K.	*Who Is the Beast*
Hall, D.	*Ox Cart Man*
Hoberman, M.	*A House Is a House for Me*
Hutchins, R.	*Rosie's Walk*
Kelley, M.	*Fall Is Not Easy*
Numeroff, L.	*If You Give a Moose a Muffin*
Numeroff, L.	*If You Give a Mouse a Cookie*
Numeroff, L.	*If You Give a Pig a Pancake*
Rylant, C.	*Long Night Moon*
Rylant, C.	*Scarecrow*
Rylant, C.	*The Relatives Came*
Schaefer, L.M.	*This Is the Rain*
Sendak, M.	*Where the Wild Things Are*
VanAllsburg, C.	*The Stranger*

Story Pyramid

Purpose

The purposes of the story pyramid instructional strategy are to:

- Motivate students to participate in story retellings.
- Provide a framework to assist students in retelling a story.
- Encourage students to think about how they can tell a story in just a few words (summarizing).

Types of Text

The story pyramid instructional strategy can be done with any narrative text. It is an excellent activity to use to introduce the idea of summarizing a text or as practice in summarizing for a postreading activity.

Steps

Preparation

1. Prepare a story pyramid frame for the story that has been read. You can use the sample frame provided or modify it, as needed, to fit the story. You can add or delete lines, depending upon the complexity of the story and the developmental level of the students.
2. Put the story pyramid frame on a chart or transparency so that it can be easily seen by all students in the group or class.

Implementation

1. If this is the first time the students have completed the activity, complete the story pyramid together, as you teach the students how to select the words that go into the frame. Since there are only a few words permitted, discuss how the selected words must be the best ones to portray the story and the characters. The goal of the activity is to help them learn to summarize, so stress that aspect of the activity; the ultimate goal is not to make a story pyramid, but to have the students learn to summarize on their own later.
2. Display the story pyramids when all the students have finished. Discuss the parts of the story that were included, and that were omitted, to support students' development of the skill of summarizing.

Basic Story Pyramid Frame

1 word describing the main character

2 words describing the main character

3 words describing the setting

4 words describing the problem or first thing that happened

5 words describing important events

6 words describing the ending

Sample Story Pyramid

Notice that the text is centered to make it look triangular in shape. This is the basis of the "pyramid" in the name of the strategy.

Cinderella

cute nice

palace house mother

her mother was dead

stepmother made her sweep floor

she went to the palace ball

she danced with the prince and ran

They got married and lived happily ever after

Story Retelling Beads

Purpose

Story retelling beads support young children as they learn to retell stories. They provide a concrete reminder of the story elements because each element is represented by a bead on a string or necklace.

Types of Text

Story retelling beads are used with narrative text because they focus on story elements.

Steps

Preparation

1. Select a simple story that lends itself to retelling and that is on an appropriate reading level for the students with whom you will be working.
2. Make a list of the story elements that you want the students to pull out of the story. List the setting and characters. Begin with the plot by just identifying the initiating event, middle event or climax, and the end.
3. For each part of the setting (time/place), characters, and plot, identify a bead that can be used to represent that element. For example, a red bird might be represented by a red bead. The forest might be represented by a green bead. You can also use figural beads if you can find them. You will need one set of beads for each student, along with a shoelace or string, depending on the size of the holes in the beads.

Implementation

1. Have the students read the story and discuss it as you normally would.
2. Give each student a baggie containing one set of beads and a string.
3. Ask the students to name the setting of the story. Discuss what bead could represent the setting and why. Put that bead on the string. Repeat this process with the characters and each of the events.
4. When the students have finished their bead strings, use the beads to retell the story. Slide a bead across the string, and state what it represents in the story. Continue on until all of the beads have been used and the whole story has been told.

Story Retelling Slide

Purpose

The story retelling slide is a manipulative tool that is used to support students' retellings of narrative text. As they slide the bead along the pipe cleaner, the pictures on the slide remind them what they need to remember to retell the text.

Types of Text

The story retelling slide is used only with narrative text since it focuses on the retelling of stories.

Steps

Preparation

1. Duplicate copies of the retelling slide on tagboard or light cardboard.
2. Punch out the holes at the top and bottom of the slide, and insert one end of a pipe cleaner in each hole.
3. Fold over about one inch of the pipe cleaner, and secure it with masking tape on the back of the slide. Slide a bead onto the open end of the pipe cleaner, and then secure that end in the same way.
4. The bead should slide freely along the pipe cleaner.

Implementation

1. After the students read a story, show them the retelling slides. Point at each image on the slide, and discuss what story element the image represents: characters, setting, and events that happened at the beginning, middle, and end of the story.
2. As you discuss each image, ask the students to tell you about that part of the story they just read. As they do so, slide the bead to the next image and have them do the same.
3. Put the students in pairs and have them retell the story they just read to each other, using the retelling slide to help them.
4. Collect the slides, and use them each time the students retell stories in the future.

Story Slide Pattern

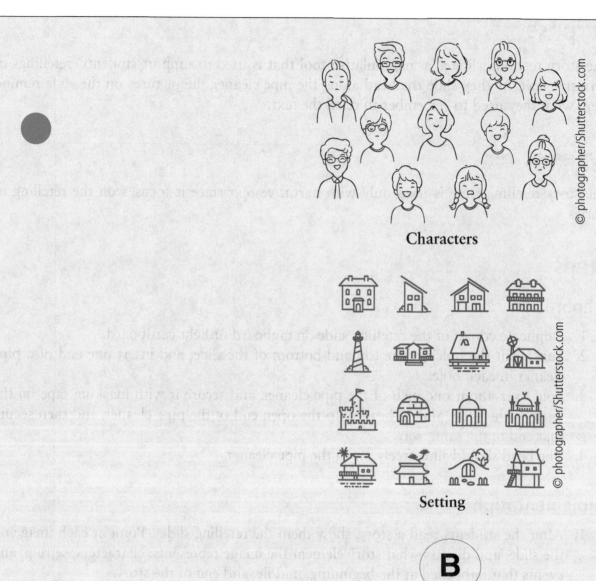

Characters

Setting

B

M

E

Story Souvenirs/Story Bits

Purpose

The purposes of the story souvenirs instructional strategy are to:

- Motivate students to participate in story retellings.
- Provide a tactile reminder of a story that was read.
- Encourage students to think about symbols that can be used to represent an entire story.

Types of Text

The story souvenirs instructional strategy can be done with any narrative text.

Steps

Preparation

1. Think about the story that the students will be reading, and identify a symbol that could be used to represent the story. It should remind students what the story was about. This will be a "story souvenir." The best souvenirs will remind the readers of characters, settings, or important events. For example, you might select a small pebble to represent *Sylvester and the Magic Pebble* by William Stieg or a seed to represent *How a Seed Grows*, by Aliki. You may choose to make paper-based souvenirs for some stories, such as a cut-out of a mouse for *Town Mouse, Country Mouse* by Jan Brett.
2. Make or gather one of these "story souvenirs" for each student who will read the story.
3. Get or make containers for each students' collection of souvenirs. Small gift bags work well for this purpose, but you can also use shoeboxes or other small containers.

Implementation

1. After the students have finished reading the story, show them the souvenir and ask them what it has to do with the story. Tell them why you selected that souvenir to represent the story.
2. Give each student one of the souvenirs to place in his or her souvenir collection. You may ask each one to summarize or retell the story for you and award the souvenir as you would a sticker for good work. If students struggle with the retelling, provide support until they can successfully retell the story and then award the souvenir.

3. After students have demonstrated that they understand how the souvenirs are chosen to represent the stories, you can have the students help you select appropriate souvenirs for subsequent stories, or you may allow them to select their own souvenir for each story that is read.

4. You may also use souvenirs that you choose to have the students predict what an upcoming story will be about.

Ways to Use the Souvenir Collections

- If you have just a few minutes and do not have time to start a new activity or lesson, have students reach into their souvenir collections and pull out one souvenir. They can then do a turn-and-talk to retell the story represented by that souvenir to a partner.

- Send the souvenir bags home at the end of each week or every two weeks for the students to use to retell the stories at home. Be sure the parents are aware of the purpose of the souvenir bags.

- Have the students draw a souvenir from their bags (without looking), and have them write a one-paragraph summary of that story.

- Have the students draw a souvenir from their bags and write a new ending for that story.

- Use the souvenir collections to line students up to leave the room. Pull out one souvenir, and the student who can correctly identify the story first may get in line. If you have more than one reading group in your classroom (resulting in different souvenir collections for the students), be sure to pull from each of the bags, as needed.

Story Tableau

Purpose

The purposes of the story tableau instructional strategy are to:

- Encourage students to "step into the shoes" of the characters in the story that is being read.
- Support students' understanding that details are important.
- Promote understanding of story sequence.
- Provide opportunities for students to express themselves creatively through the arts.

Types of Text

A story tableau activity can be completed using any narrative text.

Preparation

1. Select the text that you will use for the activity. Students should be currently reading or have already finished reading the text.
2. Select one scene from the story, and write down the page number(s) of the text that describe the scene.
3. Make a list of the characters needed in the scene.
4. Repeat the process until you have a scene in which each student can participate.

Implementation

1. Explain to the students that they will be setting up a scene from the story as if they were in a play. The difference between a tableau and a play is that no one will be talking—they are just taking a "snapshot" in time of the scene, with the characters in place, and portraying the correct emotion and activities.
2. Assign each student to a character role in one of the tableaus.
3. Students should re-read the section of the text that goes with their tableau. As a group, they should discuss where each character should be placed in the tableau, what that character should be doing, and how that character should look (facial expression) and where he or she should be looking.
4. Once the groups have their tableaus set, each group presents its tableau to the class. Once the tableau is set, the students in the remainder of the class must look carefully at the tableau to determine what is happening, what characters are involved, and how the characters are feeling. They then should try to identify the scene in the text.

5. After students are familiar with the story tableau activity, you might mix up the text assignments so that each group is presenting a tableau from a different book that was read by the class.

Extensions

1. Take a digital photograph of each tableau when all the students are in place. Display these on a bulletin board, and have students match them to the correct book/story title.
2. Have students write about what they did to portray the emotion or actions in the tableau without being able to talk or move.

Supra-segmental Phonemes

Purpose

All students should be taught about supra-segmental phonemes. These are speech sounds—inflection and stress—that impact the meaning of the text. This concept needs to be explicitly taught, particularly for English language learners.

Both word stress (accent) and sentence stress (phrasal stress) impact the meaning of speech. Word stress (accent) is included in an earlier instructional strategy.

Implementation

1. Explain to students that placing stress on different words or phrases in a sentence can drastically change the meaning.
2. Have the students read the following sentence and discuss what it means.
   I did not lose my math homework.
3. Ask the students to read the sentence again, putting stress on different words. Discuss how changing the stress changes the meaning of the sentence.
   For example:
   I did not lose my *math* homework.
   When stress is put on the word "math," the sentence means that it was homework from a different subject that was lost.

   I did not lose my math homework.
   When stress is put on the word "I," the sentence means that someone else lost the math homework.

   I did not *lose* my math homework.
   When stress is put on the word "lose," the sentence means that something else happened to the math homework.

4. Have students practice similar sentences, and explain how the meaning changes when stress is placed on different words. Transfer this to a story that is being read.

Talking Drawings

The talking drawings instructional strategy was developed by Suzanne McConnell in 1992.

Purpose

The purposes of the talking drawings activity are to:

- Activate and assess students' prior knowledge about the topic(s) of a book that you are going to read or a lesson you are going to teach.
- Motivate students and build interest in the book or topic.

Steps

Preparation

1. Read the text.
2. Select a concrete object that can be used to activate students' prior knowledge related to the text. For example, if you are reading a text about a butterfly, you might use a chrysalis or a caterpillar. If the text is about life during colonial times, you might show a butter churn.

Implementation

1. Introduce the text to the students by using the concrete item. Explain how the concrete item relates to the book. Read the title of the book. You may or may not want to show the cover of the book, as young children may simply draw what is on the cover for the activity if they have seen it.
2. Give students each a sheet of blank paper. Tell them to draw everything they know about the topic of the book. Give them at least 5 to 10 minutes to draw.
3. Have the students do a turn and talk to share their drawings with a partner. Give them about five minutes (total) for this sharing time. You may want to set a timer for two and a half minutes; when it goes off, the second person in the pair begins to share. This will make sure that both students have the same amount of time to share their drawings.

Text Connections

Encourage students to make connections before, during, and after reading. Connections are links that the students make between what they are reading and what they already know. This helps the information they are reading to be stored in the cognitive structure along with similar information and enables students to activate and use their prior knowledge to understand new information in the text.

Stress to the students that good readers make connections constantly as they are reading. The three types of connections that good readers make are as follows:

Text-to-Self

- How does this text relate to the experiences I have had?
- How does a character in this text remind me of myself?

Text-to-Text

- How does this text remind me of other stories I have read?
- How does this text remind me of movies or television shows I have seen?
- How does this text remind me of paintings I have seen or music I have heard?

Text-to-World

- How does this text relate to events I have seen in the news?
- How does this text relate to events I have read in the newspaper?

See this website for a lesson plan as well as posters about each of the text connections that you can print out and hang in your classroom:

http://www.readwritethink.org/professional-development/strategy-guides/making-connections-30659.html

Text Feature Walk

Purpose

The purposes of the text feature walk instructional strategy are to:

- Support students' reading comprehension by activating their prior knowledge before reading expository text.
- Model the processes of predicting and asking questions using text features, prior to reading expository text.
- Build students' awareness of important text features in expository text, and familiarize them with the process of looking at text features in preparation for reading.

Types of Text

The text feature walk is designed to be used with expository text.

Steps

Preparation

1. Read the text that the students will be reading, paying particular attention to text features that could be highlighted during the text feature walk.
2. Plan a think-aloud that you will use to model the process for the students. Be sure you are focusing on the important features of the text and how these features support reading comprehension.

Implementation

1. Be sure the students are familiar with the common text features in expository text.
2. Relate the text feature walk to a picture walk, with which the students should be familiar.
3. Do your planned think-aloud to model the text feature walk for the students.
4. Gradually, as you end your think-aloud, have the students begin to identify text features and explain how they will help support their understanding of the text.
5. After the text feature discussion, have the students silently read that section of the text.
6. Repeat the process with the next section of text and continue the text feature walk–reading–discussion pattern until you reach the end of the text.

7. After reading, have the students verbalize how the text feature walk helped their comprehension of the text, when they should text feature walks, and how a text feature walk is done.

Suggestions

1. Select texts for which students have adequate prior knowledge, so that they can focus on the text features during reading.
2. Use a short section of text for each part of the lesson so that students can focus on the text features in that part.
3. Review the pronunciation of new vocabulary words in the text prior to the discussion, so that students can pronounce them correctly, even if they do not yet know what they mean.
4. Use small groups to practice the text feature walks. Divide students in small groups of three to four. In their groups, students should:
   a. Select one person to start the text feature walk.
   b. That person will name the text feature (heading, map, etc.) and then read the text feature aloud for the group.
   c. As a group, students will discuss the predictions, questions, and connections that are made, based on the text features, and will discuss how they think it will relate to the main idea. All group members should participate in this discussion.
   d. A new group member should share the next feature and repeat the process. This continues until all of the text features have been discussed.

Text Features to Teach Students to Use

Name of Text Feature	Purpose of Text Feature
Title	Quickly tells the reader what information they will learn about in the text
Table of Contents	Shows students the different chapter or section titles and where they are located
Index	Directs students where to go in the text to find specific information on a topic, word, or person
Glossary	Identifies important vocabulary words for students and gives their definition
Headings or Subtitles	Help the reader identify the main idea for that section of text
Sidebars	Are set apart from the main text, usually located on the side or bottom of the page, and elaborate on a detail mentioned in the text
Pictures and Captions	Show an important object or idea from the text
Labeled Diagrams	Allow readers to see detailed depictions of an object from the text with labels that teach the important components
Charts and Graphs	Represent and show data related to, or elaborate on, something in the main body of text
Maps	Help a reader locate a place in the world that is related to the text
Cutaways and Cross Sections	Allow readers to see inside something by dissolving part of a wall or to see all the layers of an object by bisecting it for viewing
Inset Photos	Can show either a faraway view of something or a close-up shot of minute detail

This list is based on: Kelley, M. J., & Clausen-Grace, N. (2010). Guiding students through expository text with text feature walks. *The Reading Teacher, 64*(3), 191–195.

Text Pattern Graphic Organizers

Purpose

The purposes of matching text structures with graphic organizers are to:

- Support students as they organize information from expository text.
- Graphically document the relationships among information included in expository texts.
- Develop students' ability to identify types of text and the goal/purpose for reading each type.

Types of Text

Graphic organizers can be used with any type of text. This particular approach stresses the use of graphic organizers that correspond with types of expository (informational) text.

Steps

Preparation

1. Select the graphic organizer that best fits with the type of text that is being read by the students.
2. Create an anchor chart showing the graphic organizer that you will be using. You may also wish to have individual copies of the graphic organizer for individual use by the students.
3. Read the text that the students will be reading. Create a completed version of the graphic organizer to help you guide the students in completing one during the lesson.

Implementation

1. After the students have read the text silently, discuss what the author's purpose was for writing the text. Since it is expository text, the general purpose is to give information to the reader. After you have guided the students to this response, ask them if they can find a more specific reason—what kind of information is the author telling them about?
2. The students should already be familiar with the type of text structure that they are reading. After they have identified the correct text structure (cause/effect, problem/solution, generalization/description, enumeration, sequence, compare/contrast), discuss what their "job" or purpose as a reader is when reading that type of text.

3. The first time you introduce the graphic organizer, you should use a short text passage and model for the students the process of finding the text type, thinking about the reader's job, and selecting the correct graphic organizer that best displays the information from the passage. Explain how the graphic you will be using shows how the information is related. Fill in the information on the graphic organizer while you think aloud.

4. After you have modeled the process, complete the graphic organizer cooperatively with the students, so you can provide structure and guidance as they learn the process. After they are familiar with the graphic organizer, you can have the students complete the graphic organizer independently.

5. You can vary the activity by providing different levels of support for the students, as needed.

    a. Provide the passage and the graphic organizer and have the students complete the graphic organizer.

    b. Provide the passage and have the students select the correct graphic organizer for that passage from the organizers they have learned about.

    c. Provide a partially completed graphic organizer for the passage to assist students in identifying the correct placement of the information.

Text Pattern Guide

Purpose

The purposes of the text pattern guide instructional strategy are to:

- Support students' reading comprehension by making them aware of the text structure of expository texts.
- Provide students with practice using graphic organizers for taking notes from expository texts.
- Provide students with support in using graphics to visually represent textual information before they are prepared to select the graphic organizers on their own.

Types of Text

The text pattern guide is designed to be used with expository text.

Steps

Preparation

1. Select a text with an obvious text pattern (generalization/description, cause/effect, problem/solution, sequence, enumeration, comparison/contrast). Students should already be familiar with the text type and have some practice identifying that type of text.
2. Develop a graphic organizer that fits the text structure pattern on an anchor chart. Be sure the graphic you select shows the relationship(s) among the information in the text.
3. Plan how you will model the process of filling in some information from the text to give the students a good start on completing the graphic organizer.

Implementation

1. After the students finish reading the text silently, have them look for signal words in the text, and then identify the type of text pattern that is predominant in the passage.
2. Use the anchor chart to model for the students the process of finding information in the text that should be filled in to the appropriate spots in the graphic organizer. As you model, stress the relationship(s) among the information and the pattern that is represented by the text.

3. After you have filled in part of the organizer through modeling, have the students help you fill in the rest (guided practice). When they are familiar with the process and the graphic organizer, they can next complete a blank organizer that you have provided. After they are experienced with that process, move to the final stage, where the students suggest the appropriate graphic organizer for the text type and complete it individually.

Think Aloud (Modeling)

Purpose

The purposes of the think aloud instructional strategy are to:

- Provide a model of active reading for students to follow.
- Encourage students to share their thinking during reading.
- Support students' use of comprehension strategies during reading.

Types of Text

The think aloud can be done with any text. The key to an effective think aloud is to match the strategy being modeled with the text; not all texts are useful for modeling all strategies.

Steps

Preparation

1. Select the text for the think aloud. Consider what strategy/strategies you are planning to model for students, and make sure that the text provides sufficient opportunities for modeling those strategies.
2. Plan your think aloud. Select the point at which you will stop in the text, and plan exactly what you will say. Write out a *script* so that you are sure that you are modeling the strategy appropriately using the text and you do not forget to say during your modeling.

Implementation

1. A think aloud can be used as a mini-lesson or as part of a full reading lesson.
2. The teacher should read aloud from the text, stopping at the predetermined points to literally "think aloud" what he or she is thinking about the text at that point. The goal is to help students learn what "good readers do" when they are reading. The think aloud should model active, strategic reading.
3. After the teacher has modeled the implementation of the strategy by thinking aloud, the students should try it. Having them work in pairs, taking turns reading aloud and thinking aloud as they implement the strategy, is often helpful. As the students are thinking aloud, the teacher should listen to them to assess whether they are using the strategy effectively. If they are not, the teacher should do more modeling for the students.

Suggested Strategies to Model

The think aloud can be used to model almost any active reading strategy, but it lends itself very well to the following strategies:

- Clarifying difficult sentences
- Reading ahead or rereading
- Using context clues
- Using visual imagery
- Using graphic organizers
- Predicting and verifying
- Using charts, graphs, diagrams embedded in text

Think-Pair-Share and Turn and Talk

Purpose

The purposes of a turn and talk or think-pair-share activity are to:

- Activate and assess students' prior knowledge about the topic(s) of a book that you are going to be reading.
- Motivate students and build interest in the book.
- Involve all students in the prereading text discussion.
- Allow students to build prior knowledge about the text topic by listening to their peers.

Types of Text

Turn and talk and think-pair-share may be used effectively with all types of text or with lessons in any content area.

Steps

Preparation

1. Read the text.
2. Identify a main concept or topic that students should know about before reading the text. For example, if you are reading a book about weather, the topic might be tornados or hurricanes.
3. Brainstorm a list of important features or facts about the topic that you think the students should know in order to read and understand the text.

Implementation: Turn and Talk

1. Introduce the book to the students. Show them the cover and read the title.
2. Ask the students to turn and talk for one minute to a partner about the topic you have selected. You should say something like: "Think about what you know about tornados. Turn to your partner and tell that person three things you know about tornados. Then listen to that person tell you what he or she knows about tornados."
3. As the students talk, you listen for the important concepts/facts that you have identified. Note which students seem to have little information about the concept.

4. Call on several students to share information that they know about the topic. These should be the students who shared some of the important concepts/facts that you identified about the text.

5. If none of the students shared the concepts/facts you identified, you should share those with the students.

Implementation: Think-Pair-Share

1. Think-pair-share is basically the same as turn and talk. Some teachers use think-pair-share when they have students working in groups of four. The students "think" and then they "pair" to share their thoughts with a partner. Finally, they "share" with the entire group.

2. Think-pair-share can also be adapted into "write-pair-share."

Unlikely Pairs

Purpose

The purposes of the unlikely pairs instructional strategy are to:

- Encourage students to pay close attention to images and the feelings evoked by particular colors and designs.
- Develop students' skills in making intertextual connections.
- Provide opportunities for students to express themselves creatively through the arts.

Types of Text

Unlikely pairs can be completed using any images. There are numerous websites that can be used for locating a wide variety of images and visual artwork.

Steps

Preparation

1. Select two images that you would put together as an "unlikely pair."
2. Plan what you will say to the students for your *think aloud* to model the process of identifying two images that will "go together" in a particular way.
3. Find several sets of images that can be put together into pairs. Make one set of images for each group of students.

Implementation

1. Read the book *Unlikely Pairs* by Bob Raczka to the students, showing them the pairs in the book and taking time to talk about how the pictures "go together" and why they are amusing and "unlikely."
2. Give the students the image sets you created in advance, and have them pair up the images into unlikely pairs. As they are working, go from group to group (or pair to pair) of students and have them explain their thinking for you on at least one or two of their paired images to make sure that they are on the right track.
3. Once you think they have gotten the idea, provide website access or provide printouts of a large number of images and have students individually create an unlikely pair.

4. Students should respond to the following questions, either in writing or orally, about the pair that was created:
   a. What is it about the two images that make them go together?
   b. How is the pair "unlikely"? (What makes it amusing or unexpected to see the two images together?)

What Book?

Purpose

The What Book? activity is designed to build students' visual literacy by encouraging them to look very closely at images. It also can be used to build an understanding of characters.

Types of Text

What Book? is used with any paintings that include people reading books.

Steps

Preparation

1. Select an image of a painting that includes someone reading a book.
2. Prepare a sample response that you can share with the students. Answer the questions:
   - What book is this person reading?
   - What makes you think so?
   - What is it about the person's clothing that gave you clues?
   - What is it about the setting that gave you clues?
   - What is it about the book itself that gave you clues?
   - Did the colors used by the artist help you decide on the book? Why?

Implementation

1. Show the painting to the students.
2. Tell the students that you are curious about what book the person in the painting is reading. Tell them the title of the book that you selected, and explain your choice, using information from the painting to support your book choice.
3. Show some other paintings that include books. Allow the students to select a painting for the activity. Their job is to decide for themselves what book the person is reading and explain their reasoning.
4. Share the responses. Stress that there is not a right or wrong answer, but they need to support their reasoning with details from the painting.

Paintings that Contain Books

The Artist's Wife with a Book (Schmidt)
https://artsandculture.google.com/asset/the-artist-s-wife-with-a-book/_QHxxbwf5X0Iog

Brother Gregorio Belo of Vicenza (Lotto)
https://www.metmuseum.org/art/collection/search/436917

Young Girl Reading (Fragonard)
https://www.nga.gov/collection/art-object-page.46303.html

Reading Lesson (Toulmouche)
https://www.mfa.org/collections/object/reading-lesson-32101

Portrait of a Boy Reading (Reynolds)
https://www.niceartgallery.com/Sir-Joshua-Reynolds/Portrait-Of-A-Boy-Reading-oil-painting.html

Boy Reading (Kennington)
https://www.the-athenaeum.org/art/detail.php?ID=58085

Word Building with Letter Cubes

Purpose

Students will blend sounds of letters in CVC words.

Preparation

1. Assemble the cubes or write letters on purchased wooden or foam cubes.
   Cube 1: Letters *t, d, c, b, f, m* Cube 2: Letters *a, e, i, o, u, i* (2 sides with i) Cube 3: Letters *n, m, d, b, r, s*. Be sure to put a line under letters that can be confused if read upside down—for example <u>d</u> <u>b</u> <u>u</u>. You can change the letters, but always check in advance that words can be made with the letters you choose.
2. Prepare game mats for each student. Laminate the mats so that they can be reused.

Implementation

1. Students can play the game in small groups of two to four. Each group needs three cubes: 1 cube #1 with vowels, 1 cube #2 with initial consonants, and 1 cube #3 with final consonants. Each student needs a game mat and an erasable thin-tip marker.
2. Model the activity for the students the first time they play so that they understand how the game works. Be sure they understand the difference between "real words" and "nonsense words."
3. Students take turns rolling the cubes. They should roll the cubes in order (1, 2, 3). As each cube is rolled, the student places it on the mat on the correct number (1, 2, 3). (Note: If you want, you can make the letters on each cube correspond with the color of the number on the game mat so that the students will have support in getting the correct cube in the correct place.)
4. The student reads the word. If it is a real word, the student writes it in the "real words" column. If it is a nonsense word, the student writes it in the "nonsense words" column.
5. The student passes the cubes to the next student in the group, who repeats the process. You can give the students a certain amount of time to play, or you may indicate that each one should have a certain number of turns (six turns, for example).

Cubes

Real Words	Nonsense Words

Word Detectives

Purpose

The purposes of the word detectives instructional strategy are to:

- Encourage students to be curious about how words originated.
- Encourage students to use analogy when identifying unknown words (looking for similarities among words).
- Encourage students to use the dictionary and other word resources in order to research word origins.

Types of Text

The word detectives instructional strategy can be used with either fiction or nonfiction text.

Steps

Preparation and Implementation

1. On a daily basis, you should model for students that you are interested in words and what they mean. Bring in interesting words that you find in your reading, and share them with your students.
2. Model for students how to use word resources such as the dictionary, thesaurus, websites, and the encyclopedia to research word etymologies (word origins).
3. Develop a word wall, bulletin board, or class book of unique and interesting words. Encourage students to bring in words they find in their reading to add to the class collection.

Suggestions

1. Have a "word of the week" to introduce your students to colorful and interesting words. Try to take the words from class readings or books related to topics that the class is studying in the content areas (science, social studies, mathematics, etc.)
2. Have a "magic word" for the day. Select a unique word to teach the class on Monday. For the rest of the week, any time the students find the word in text or use it correctly in their classroom conversation or discussion, they earn a point for the class. If the class reaches the class goal by Friday, they get a special treat—perhaps a special read aloud by a guest reader!

Recommended Sources for Unique Words and Etymological Information

Websites

Online Etymology Dictionary   http://www.etymonline.com/

Etymologically Speaking   http://www.westegg.com/etymology/

Selected Etymology

http://www.fun-with-words.com/etym_example.html

Word Origins

http://www.wordorigins.org/index.php/big_list/

Books

Baker, R.F. *In a Word: 750 Words and Their Origins*

Hyperion Books for Children. *A Chartreuse Leotard in a Magenta Limousine and Other Words Named After People and Places*

Wuffson, D.L. *Abracadabra to Zombie: More Than 500 Wacky Word Origins*

Word Plays

Purpose

The purposes of the word plays instructional strategy are to:

- Encourage students to make connections between vocabulary and story elements.
- Promote vocabulary learning with an activity that utilizes kinesthetic and dramatic activities to involve the students in the word meanings.
- Support the transfer of new vocabulary terms from students' reading vocabularies to their speaking vocabularies.

Types of Text

The word plays instructional strategy uses lists of words that can be drawn from or inspired by any narrative text.

Steps

Preparation

1. Select a cluster of words from a fiction text that students will be reading. The words should give the impression of some aspects of the story elements: setting, characters, problem/goal, actions, resolution, and feeling.
2. Write each word on a card. On the back of the card, note the name of the story. This will be helpful if the cards are ever mixed up with cards from a different story.
3. If you make several cards from the same story, you can divide the students into small groups for the activity. Each group gets a different set of cards from the same story. It is interesting to compare the skits that are actually based on the same text.

Implementation

1. Each group of students receives a set of cards from the story. Their task is to construct a three-minute skit based on the vocabulary words.
2. Model the planning process for the students before you expect them to do it on their own. Show them how to think about each word in order to identify whether it is about the setting, character, problem, and so on. This will help them plan their skits.

3. Give the students at least 10 to 15 minutes to plan their skits. The goal is for them to try to predict what the story will be about and to utilize the vocabulary words in their skits.

4. List all the words from all the groups on a chart, or use the cards in a pocket chart. After all the skits have been presented, have the students discuss the similarities and differences among the skits to make predictions about the text before they actually read the story. Encourage them to use the vocabulary words in their discussion and predictions.

Word Theater

Purpose

Word theater builds oral reading fluency. After the students have already read a text at least once silently, you can use word theater to encourage them to reread the text repeatedly. This activity works very effectively to build students' reading rate. In addition, it assists in building vocabulary.

Steps

Preparation

1. Select a portion of the text (several pages at most) to use for the activity.
2. Select words from the target text, and write them on index cards. They should be words that can easily be acted out. Write the page number and the sentence from the text, with the target word underlined or in a different color to make it stand out.
3. On the back of each card, write the name of the book in which the word is found. This will come in handy if the card sets from several books are mixed up and you need to sort them out.

Implementation

1. Tell the students what page(s) you will be using from the text for the activity. Have them turn to those pages in the book so that they are ready for the activity.
2. Students take turns choosing a card and then acting out the secret word for the group.
3. Students in the group must read through the target text *as quickly as they can* to find the *secret word*. When they think they have it, they raise their hands and point to the word in the text. Watch to see who finds the word first but wait until almost all the students have found the word in the text before you call on anyone. This will ensure that even the slower readers will read through the text and will have had the repeated reading practice.
4. The student who finds the word first (*and who is pointing to the word in the text*) reads the sentence containing the word aloud from the text. If he or she is correct, he or she goes next (or if he or she has already had a turn, can select the next student) to act out a word.

Sample Word Theater Word Card

(front)

p. 15

clutching

Ramona ran down the street,
clutching her bookbag.

(back)

Ramona Quimby, Age 8

Write the Letter

Purpose

The purposes of the write the letter instructional strategy are to:

- Develop students' visual literacy skills.
- Encourage students to "step into a character's shoes" to see things from the character's perspective.
- Look carefully at details and how they build characterization.
- Help students understand the idea of "voice" in writing.

Types of Text

The write the letter strategy is designed to be used with any visual image that portrays a letter writer or letter reader. Suggested visual texts include the following:

The Letter (**Cassatt**)
https://www.abacus-gallery.com/oil-painting/1285054068/Mary-Cassatt/The-Letter-1891.html

Reading the Letter (**Picasso**)
http://www.pablopicasso.net/reading-the-letter/

Two Women Reading a Letter on a Couch (**Reggianini**)
http://vintageprintable.swivelchairmedia.com/art-and-design/portrait-painting-women-reading-
  a-letter-on-a-couch/

Girl Reading a Letter by Candlelight with a Young Man Peering over Her Shoulder (**Wright**)
http://en.wikipedia.org/wiki/File:Joseph_Wright_of_Derby._Girl_Reading_a_Letter_by_Candlelight,_
  With_a_Young_Man_Peering_over_Her_Shoulder._c.1760-62.jpg

Reading the Letter (**Gerard**)
http://www.artsunlight.com/artist-NG/N-G0025-Marguerite-Gerard/N-G0025-0015-reading-the-
  letter-panel.html

Little Boy Writing a Letter (**Rockwell**)
http://www.wikipaintings.org/en/norman-rockwell/little-boy-writing-a-letter-1920

Woman in Blue Reading a Letter (**Vermeer**)
http://herbgreene.org/GREENE%20IMAGES/Paintings/ARTISTS/VERMEER.html

The Love Letter (**Vermeer**)
http://herbgreene.org/GREENE%20IMAGES/Paintings/ARTISTS/VERMEER.html

Woman Writing a Letter (**Vermeer**)
http://herbgreene.org/GREENE%20IMAGES/Paintings/ARTISTS/VERMEER.html

Goodbye Letters on the Bridge (**Brady**)
http://www.spraygraphic.com/ViewProject/779/normal.html

Steps

Preparation

1. Select the paintings (texts) that the students will be reading. Have at least three to four letters from a diverse group of paintings.
2. Do some background research about the artist so that you can introduce the paintings to the students.

Implementation

1. Introduce the activity to the students by using a painting that will not be part of the writing activity. Model for them how you "read" the painting by looking at all of the details in the background, the type of clothing, the setting, the expressions of the characters, and so on. Be sure to discuss the presentation of the letter (one of the writing traits)—what material would the letter be written on? What type of ink would be used? What handwriting style? What will the content of the letter be about?
2. As a class, write one letter together as a model. Emphasize that the students are stepping into the shoes of the letter reader/writer and should make the letter sound as much as possible like the voice of the person who is writing it.
3. Each student selects one of the paintings that you have chosen for the activity. The task is for the student to write the letter that is seen in the painting. Students should try to make the letter *look* like the one that would be seen in the painting by using the correct type of materials, font, handwriting, and so on that would be seen with the letter in the painting.
4. They should write the title of the painting (or an identifying letter or number that you have assigned to each painting) on the *back* of their letter. In addition, students should write a paragraph explaining their choices for the letter, using evidence from the painting to support their choices in content and presentation.
5. Post the letters on a bulletin board along with the paintings. Number each letter. The task will be for the students to match the letters with the paintings that inspired them.

Write the Story of the Picture

Purpose

The purposes of the write the story of the picture instructional strategy are to:

- Encourage students to pay close attention to details in illustrations.
- Have students utilize images to inspire creative writing.
- Provide opportunities for students to express themselves creatively through the arts.

Types of Text

Write the story of the picture can be completed using any image, especially those that show emotions, interesting events, or unusual situations that will inspire creative writing.

Steps

Preparation

1. Select an image (photograph, painting, print) that will inspire students' writing.
2. Using a different image, prepare a sample that you can use to model the process for students. Write the story that you are inspired to write from the image.

Implementation

1. Show the students the sample image you selected for your modeling. Ask them what they notice about the image. Encourage them to use strong descriptive words that portray emotion and verbs that suggest action.
2. Do a think aloud as you look at the image, and then read the story you wrote about the image to the students.
3. Ask them to tell you ways that your story related to the image. Stressing the connections between the story and the images, colors, shapes, and emotions portrayed in the picture is critical.
4. Show the students the picture they will be using for their assignment.
5. Ask them what they notice about that picture, and have them write a story inspired by the picture.
6. Display the picture with the stories it inspired.

Variation

After your modeling, provide a variety of images from which the students can choose. When each student has selected an image and written a story, make the images/stories into an interactive bulletin board. Can the class read the stories and match them to the image that inspired them?